FIRE
IN THE
STRAW

BOOKS BY NICK LYONS

The Seasonable Angler
Jones Very: Selected Poems (editor)
Fisherman's Bounty (editor)
The Sony Vision
Locked Jaws
Fishing Widows
Two Fish Tales
Bright Rivers
Confessions of a Fly-Fishing Addict
Trout River (text for photographs by Larry Madison)
Spring Creek
A Flyfisher's World
My Secret Fish-Book Life
Sphinx Mountain and Brown Trout
Full Creel
In Praise of Wild Trout (editor)
Hemingway's Many-Hearted Fox River
The Quotable Fisherman (editor)
Classic Fishing Stories (editor)
Hemingway on Fishing (editor)
Traver on Fishing (editor)
Best Fishing Stories (editor)
Fishing Stories
Fire in the Straw

FIRE
IN THE
STRAW

NOTES ON INVENTING A LIFE

NICK LYONS

Arcade Publishing • New York

Arcade Publishing books may be purchased in bulk at special discounts for sales promotion, corporate gifts, fund-raising, or educational purposes. Special editions can also be created to specifications. For details, contact the Special Sales Department, Arcade Publishing, 307 West 36th Street, 11th Floor, New York, NY 10018 or arcade@skyhorsepublishing.com.

Arcade Publishing® is a registered trademark of Skyhorse Publishing, Inc.®, a Delaware corporation.

Visit our website at www.arcadepub.com.

10 9 8 7 6 5 4 3 2 1

Library of Congress Cataloging-in-Publication Data is available on file.

Cover design by Liz Driesbach
Cover photograph credit: istockphoto/borchee

Print ISBN: 978-1-951627-19-5
Ebook ISBN: 978-1-951627-20-1

Printed in the United States of America

Some chapters appeared previously, usually in other forms, as follows:
The Antioch Review: "Detachment" and "A Reluctant Publisher"
Take it to the Hoop, A Basketball Anthology: "The Last Game"
Big Sky Journal: "Mari, Montana, the Sphinx, and Me"
The Pennsylvania Gazette: "Those Woodstock Summers"

for MARI
(1935–2016)

and for
Paul (1958–2018), Charlie, Jenny, and Tony
without whom I would have had no life

"... the tiger, though he hide his claws will at last discover his rapine; the lion's looks are not the maps of his meaning.... Fire cannot be hid in the straw, nor the nature of man so concealed but at last it will have his course."
—Thomas Lodge, *Rosalynde*

Oh what a thing is man! how farre from power,
From setled peace and rest!
He is some twentie sev'rall men at least
Each sev'rall houre.
—George Herbert, "Giddinesse"

CONTENTS

CONTENTS

ACKNOWLEDGMENTS

Warm thanks to my daughter, and agent, Jennifer Lyons, for her early and unwavering faith in this book, and for valuable suggestions, and to my son Tony for publishing it.

A number of people have been especially helpful during the final stages of seeing this book travel from manuscript to finished book and it is a pleasure to acknowledge their help. I thank Kristin Crawford for her careful typing of my manuscript—and, simultaneously, for her many thoughtful corrections and editorial suggestions. Bonnie Thompson remains one of the most exacting of copyeditors—and she too added important editorial changes. Lilly Golden, who edited this book, and saw it through the many stages of production, proved once again that she is an author's best friend. I'm very grateful to all of the above.

FOREWORD

I have long been intensely curious about the parts of any life—
its various beginnings, its twists and turns, where, finally, it settled, if ever. The journey is rarely neat, mostly messy, if seen
closely. No arc invites such intense scrutiny as one's own. After
a certain age, we remember those details that want most to be
remembered but rarely, until xperhaps late in the story, see the
pattern they have built. Often the details resist becoming a pattern but remain disparate, not to be yoked by any power,
prompted by chance, by the time in one's life, what one had for
dinner.

Except for a moment or two, my life I suspect is rather
ordinary in its details—and I have persuaded myself to write
about parts of it in this brief book only for several reasons: the
selfish one of wanting—sometimes desperately—to understand
what I did and what happened to me, what it might mean and

why, and in the thought that some of my odd journey will interest people who have lived with similar events and strivings.

I began to write sections of these recollections a full sixty-odd years ago in a little room I lived in after a few years in the Army, in Greenwich Village. At first I had raw notes on bits of paper and in a journal I began to keep; then there were stories about some episodes in my life and some of these became an ill-fated novel with a thinly disguised and too familiar central figure. When I began to write personal essays—some "straight" and some "piscatorial"—I found a voice I could use for the rest of my life. Sections of some of those essays appear almost intact in this book; some overlap or connect; some parts at first may conjure a different author, which I probably was. In the end, I wanted a narrative that sought to follow the arc of my life.

My friend Herbert Leibowitz wrote a wonderful book on American autobiography called *Fabricating Lives,* which is what mostly happens. No biography or autobiography tells either the whole story or the truly accurate story. In the selection of detail and choice of anecdote I have no doubt simmered in mendacity and rigged my own tale, though my words have pleaded for responsibility. And there is so much I have omitted—especially about my beloved wife and four children, and my grandchildren, whom I have loved so long and passionately and cannot write about sensibly.

But I have tried to hew close to what I thought was true, even as I explored, as I pressed into my mid-eighties, my varied life, in some of its defining parts.

Nick Lyons
Woodstock, New York
July 2019

FIRE
IN THE
STRAW

1

BOARDING AWAY

We lived in a labyrinthine apartment on Walton Avenue in the Bronx, my grandparents, my two bachelor uncles, my mother, and me, and the place was redolent of chopped liver and gefilte fish and pickled herring, and the sounds of Yiddish were always in my ears, and my mother was rarely there. Grandpa was a bearded patriarch who spoke little and applied salves and gauze to his calves every morning. Grandma frequently used the hand grinder attached to the kitchen table and did all the cooking; my uncles Jack and Dave were up early, back late but always had words and a smile for me. I had my own little room and was very content in the big apartment.

My grandparents and my uncles were my world and they never raised their voices and always smiled or said something funny. Much later, a cousin told me they were "spoiling me rotten."

One September day my mother and Uncle Dave said we were going for a drive. Grandma gave me a plate of cucumbers and roast chicken—my favorite foods; she'd left the cucumbers thick and the chicken white and cold, precisely how I liked them. "You know I don't like you," Grandma said, pinching my cheek, her little joke. I wiped away the pinch, as I always did. Grandpa nodded his great white head gravely, then turned away when I put on my navy-blue cap and cheerily said good-bye for the afternoon; Louis Bernstein was a man of few English words. This was 1937. I was five. We were just going for a short trip in my mother's Dodge. The license plate was 4U444.

I was skinny and freckled and had a queasy feeling when we got to a gray gabled building. I held my mother's hand fiercely as we entered, watched a valise that suddenly appeared vanish into another room, and looked up at a white-haired and ramrod-straight Miss Burt. She had known a lot of little boys like me. She knew precisely how to handle them. Did I like toys? I admitted, to her question, that I did. So she took me into a back room and there were metal trains, rag dolls, foot-long wooden blocks, paints, crayons, a red playhouse that you could climb right into, and lots of colorful books. My mother and Uncle Dave, she assured me, would still be there when I came back. They nodded as I shyly took Miss Burt's firm hand: they would still be there.

The old lady closed the door and then showed me how the trains worked, and I piled two stacks of wooden blocks to a height of three feet and with her help put a large block across them for an arch. I looked at the door several times. My mother would still be there. She had said so.

But she was not. When this was clear, I kicked and clawed, screamed as loud and long as I could, then pounded the floor with my feet like machine-gun fire. In a short while, the weight of my fury choking me, my voice grew hoarse and my limbs went bloodless. I could not believe that she had left me there alone. What had I done to deserve this?

My time at the Burt School was neither out of Dickens nor at all like Edward Dahlberg's in *Because I Was Flesh*; the school was a perfectly decent place, several teachers were warm and wise, but during those first long nights, alone in the dark, I promptly began to water the bedsheets; I also began to get dull, binding pressures through my ribs and thought my heart would bust out of my chest. Confrontation would not get me out, I soon saw, nor would screaming or bed-wetting, which stopped. The chest pains gnawed at me at their pleasure and lasted thirty years, give or take a few.

The school itself was a dark Victorian building, with innumerable dark gray hallways, dark old landscape paintings, heavy curtains, and a great porch around its exterior. About half the students—those under seven—slept in one huge room. In the night, after we had all said, "Now I lay me," kneeling on the floor beside our beds in our Dr. Dentons—"if I should die before I wake, I pray the Lord my soul to take"—after the lights were out and we were left to our own thoughts, I could hear the low cries and whimpers and waited for one of the teachers to come in, glance around, listen, the room suddenly silent, and then leave. And then the night sounds would start again. My sounds—the crash and shout of my brain, the chest thuds, the abject loneliness—were inaudible. The enemy held all the aces. Now, in the clutch of old age, I still feel the images of that place in my half-waking dreams, as starkly as if they had occurred that morning. And I still discover, when I am betrayed by a friend or an associate, when I am lied to outright, when someone insults one of my children or grandchildren, I still feel the tattoos of that place on the walls of my brain. For those days remain crouched inside me, and though I only spent three years there, the measured waiting that became my chief strategy lasted well into adulthood, and the weapons and strengths I later found were often compensations. I saw my mother only on occasional weekends, and I spoke to her increasingly with more caution and care and began to live more and more in the cave of my own brain.

Each morning we were required to sit on a small porcelain potty and if we delivered nothing after trying for a third day we were given an enema. Silent and sober lessons in gray little classrooms took six hours each day—the Burt School was well known for its academic strictness—and I had another hour for piano lessons in the musty cupboard of a room on the fourth floor. There the metronome tick-tocked back and forth, like my heart, beating me to the punch every hour, and I felt my disharmony with the music as Miss Clarke, who also taught English, said, "No, Nicki. Too slow. Nicki, you're rushing." She was small and compact and always fair, and by the end of my third year I had learned enough piano to give one recital, under duress and disastrously, at the hotel my grandfather owned, the Laurel House—it was late in the summer I left Burt's, to a packed house, and I have never played a note since.

In the afternoons and on weekends, we had a few hours of free time or "Recreation." I was taken to see the *Hindenburg* fly overhead, the remains of the Danbury Hat Factory after the great fire, and long drives on Sunday afternoons, five or six of us packed into the huge school Buick, once to a local castle, several times to nearby lakes with sand beaches. Often we took walks. One route led through the fields and woods to that small body of water called Ice Pond. It had been used by Revolutionary War troops to gather their ice; later, ice from the pond was cut into thick rectangles and shipped commercially throughout Westchester County. It was simply a pond of a few acres, clear enough but never so translucent as spring ponds I later saw in the West, set into a concave landscape like some jewel, brilliantly alive with reflections of sun on its flat or ruffled surface. I did not fish it at first, but by mid-autumn, with the leaves golden and scarlet on the birches and oaks and umber leaves floating on the pond, I knew nothing more beautiful or mysterious. A few months later it was solid as stone and slippery, and we ran and slid on it and the older kids brought their skates.

That spring I began to fish in the pond. Like Aksakov, the Russian memoirist, after the first day of it I was at once mad for fishing. I used a long branch of ash, stripped of its bark, and seven or eight feet of green cord onto which I tied a red-and-white float, and snelled hooks purchased in Peekskill from my twenty-cents-a-week allowance, paid to me at exactly five o'clock every Friday afternoon. Near the edges of the pond I sometimes heard, then saw, a frog, and in the depths there were the pancake shapes of the sunfish, unhurried, their gills pulsing, their white puckered mouths opening and closing to some purpose I could not imagine. Standing alone for hours, like a crane or heron, alone but somehow never lonely here, silent, I was mesmerized by the way the lines and planes of light angled down toward some strange matrix near the sandy bottom, a region numinous and wild. And I caught sunfish, tiger-striped perch, a few bullheads with broad and whiskered mouths, and an occasional rock bass in the little lukewarm pond, a world. I loved every moment of it: threading a tough little garden worm onto the hook so that it covered the point and left part of the bait wriggling; watching the bobber intently for any movement other than that caused by the waves; judging beforehand whether I had a pecking sunny, a bold perch, or a whiskered catfish on my line—or even a larger rock bass or black bass or the rare snakelike pickerel. I loved the bright colors of the fish, their dogged fight, the suspense of casting my bait into the waters and waiting for some little creature from that other realm to meet my invitation. I liked the shock and surprise when a fish took my bait, when my bobber trembled, even slightly.

At the pond I found a link to some world beyond that of my frozen affections, my anxiety, my sadness. My eyes were riveted to that red-and-white bobber, tipping back and forth, then darting down, and by the mystical geometries of light in water, the inverted cone within those depths, where, somewhere, were those endlessly interesting creatures who could live and breathe in water.

I have never been able to explain to those who asked me why I love to fish—first with worms in that sump of a pond, then in the creek below South Lake at the Laurel House, where I went every summer. Eventually and for many years, I fished with long delicate rods and tiny flies. Mostly I have dodged the question, but if there is a reason for my passion it is to be found in those days on Ice Pond and in South Lake. There, my eyes and ears keyed to water, float, and sound, I felt fully alive. There I felt an electric connection not only to a fish on the line but to all those things that made such an event possible—bait and tackle, shadows and reflections on the water, trees and cattails and frogs, opaque worlds beneath the surface, and the fish themselves. There I touched something larger perhaps, more momentous than myself, and there, most fully, I forgot myself, the Burt School, my mother. Fishing always had a disproportionately haunting effect on me.

Eventually I made a few friends: Billy, a year older, with whom I played War and Commando in the woods and with whom I sometimes fished, and little dark-haired Nancy, with whom we played House.

For a few weeks House was our favorite game. We played it behind the gigantic oak a short way up the hill. Nancy was always the Mommy; Billy and I took turns being Daddy or Doctor or Child. We probably showed a little flesh, and we may even have touched some now and then along with our interminable chatter. I remember nothing more but there must have been more because of what happened. None of us believed we had any real family anymore so we became very close and House was our own secret. We played every afternoon we could sneak away, for several weeks, behind the huge oak.

Of course Miss Burt found out and summoned Mr. Prince, the arithmetic teacher. I was held bare-assed in the high white bed in the infirmary, with all the other teachers standing nearby, and that doubled-over belt descended with its searing sting, over and over, and I felt my buttocks tighten and my teeth bite down on my lips until I tasted blood, and then I lay shaking and exposed, there on the white sheets, and Miss Burt said in her firm voice, "That will be all, Mr. Prince."

Nancy and I did not even nod after that, and she left before the end of the term. Billy and I had little enough to say to each other but we were both in school for another two years and eventually we spoke, though never of that incident, and in the fall we began to fish together again.

I tried to be a good student, and even when I wasn't able to concentrate on a book, I tried to look as if I were. My mind wandered, sometimes to the pond, sometimes into a vast field of mystery about who I was and whether I had a father, how I was supposed to behave, which made my chest hurt and my brain burn, and all of my report cards, in and after the Burt School, advised that I "could do better." Still, I tried always to look as if I was doing the best I could; being good, being very good, doing what adults wanted me to do, I thought, would lead them to hurt me less. Survival. That's what it was about. And didn't I know a lot about that already? I knew more about that lean figure on the crossed beams than any of the Christian children, that anguished wooden figure in the Catholic church, high over the altar.

The first time I entered that cavernous room, its ceilings miles high, so unlike the claustrophobic little synagogue I went to with Grandpa, I felt twice as small as I'd ever felt. The space was immense. As we walked down the aisle, I looked at the windows of many colors against the walls, lit from the sun. And then, just before I was asked to kneel, something I'd never done except when I said, "Now I lay me," I saw the huge, nearly naked man, his arms outstretched, the nails, his tilted head with a crown of leaves, the blood, his legs together, the spike.

Miss Burt put her finger to her mouth; we must be perfectly quiet. Had I gasped? What had he done to deserve that? And who was he?

As the words of the costumed man on the stage droned on, half music, half incantation, in a language I could not understand, my eyes flitted to the endless space above me, where the sun illuminated brilliant stained-glass windows on which there were figures with rings of silver or gold above each head, babies with wings. But my gaze always went back, tentatively at first, to the mammoth figure directly in front of me, and in twenty minutes, when I realized that he would not turn me to stone, I looked neither to the right nor the left. I looked at nothing other than him. The man was alive. The nails were through his hands, the blood was real, the crown was of thorns not leaves, and that single spike pinned both feet below the ankle to the base of the beam. There was blood everywhere, on his forehead, on the palms and wrists of his hands, on his feet. My face burned. My right hand gripped the arm of the pew in front of me as hard as it could. I turned toward the student next to me. He did not look scared. In fact, he looked more peaceful than I'd ever seen him. So I tried to listen to the great reverberating sounds of the organ, watch the pantomime of the strangely clothed men in front of me, now chanting, now swinging an object on a chain in front of them. I tried to make some sense of the aureate pageantry, so much more compelling and magnificent than what happened in that small, dark shul at which Grandpa prayed, rocking back and forth as he did, a blue-and-white shawl with tassels over his shoulders, the black cap on his head. I understood not a word of either but the language was warmer, more emotional, than the cold metallic tones I heard in the great church.

I went there several Sundays, each time trying to understand what everyone there was doing, what they were asking for—terrified, haunted, compelled to watch that man alive on the wooden cross, the man who must know more than anyone about survival and pain. When my mother visited for the first time, I told her in great detail about the man on the cross and she told Miss Burt that I was not to go to that place anymore, and I never did, ever, instead spending Sunday mornings with the cook.

THE YEARS PASSED, now blurred, with irregular visits from my mother in her Dodge, sometimes with Uncle Dave or Uncle Jack but never my grandparents. Mama did not change. She looked very beautiful to me in her colorful dresses and floppy hats. I had longed to be close to her, but now I shied from hugging or kissing her. She always wanted to know how my schoolwork had progressed, and I told her as best I could, and her warm manner made her popular with the other students and with the teachers. She knew how to be liked, and seemed to like beyond all else to be liked by others. But I could not hug her or kiss her and I'm sure she felt this, and I rarely could do either when we both grew older and I had my own family. I learned from her how to become involved in the lives of others, to ask them questions and smile at their wit. I do not know now, a full eighty years later, whether all that is an act of heart, for which we both have been praised, or an act of rank hypocrisy.

Mama, with the little hop in her walk and her perpetual smile, brought three or four gentleman friends up to visit during my third year at the Burt School. Several times she came with her unmarried friend Neale and her son Clifford, a quiet boy only months younger than me. There was a very thin man, with fish-belly-white pinched cheeks, and a man I later learned was called Jesse W. Eric, a handsome man thirty years older than Mama, with a handlebar mustache, very deferential and warm to my mother. He came twice. There was something mysterious about it all and it remained a mystery to me until I realized one morning on my way to the pond that maybe I had gotten to the Burt School in the first place because I didn't have a father and my mother had to work, and just maybe my mother wanted to marry one of these visitors. I told Billy my theory that she wanted to marry them and he said, "Not all of them," which made sense. We were headed to the pond and when we got there I took a worm from a peach can and threaded it carefully onto the hook and flipped out the line. We were both standing quietly, knee-deep in Ice Pond, watching our bobbers, and I thought about it all, and he asked: "Look, do you want to get out of this place?"

Did he mean that we should go over the fence, like Greg, the ten-year-old, had? I remembered the affair well: the phone calls, the scurry of teachers; Miss Burt's grim face and agitated voice; two state troopers bringing poor Greg into the living room like an escaped convict at nine-thirty the next morning. It did not look like much fun.

"You're nearly eight years old," said Billy, "and you don't know nothing yet. Do you want to stay here until you're an old man or do you want to leave this place forever and live in a house like everyone else in the world?"

I concentrated on the bobber, which twitched back and forth with the waves. Not even a sunny. Without turning my eyes, I said to him: "Nobody gets out of this place."

"Help her, dummy," my friend said. "This is your big chance. She's just begging for you to like one of them. Then she'll marry him and you'll get out of this place. It's *that* simple, Nicki."

An opportunity presented itself two weekends later.

The new man was young, younger than my mother. This was a good sign. We played catch with one of the school softballs, and he had a way of winding up before he threw the ball that was terrifically funny. He also showed a remarkable interest in fishing. We went to Ice Pond together and pretty soon he was holding my hand and asking all sorts of questions about what I caught in the pond and how big they were and what did I use for bait. I instructed him as best I could, given his obvious ignorance of fishing, for he seemed truly interested. When we got there he did not say anything, not even a small scold, when I walked right into the pond in my brown-and-tan shorts and shirt and began to fish. And he had a perfectly marvelous response when I flipped out a modest little perch. He even offered to help take it off the hook, which I refused. He seemed to like me and I was beginning very much to want people to like me, though I did not like the way he raised a camera as I turned from the pond and snapped my picture. There was something sneaky about that—and I've never liked my picture taken.

But his arm was around my shoulder when we walked back from the pond to meet Mama, who had been talking to my teachers, and we were chattering away like old friends—which was not precisely the case. When Mama saw us, she said, "I see you boys had a great time fishing."

Billy was a genius. Two weeks later—in the middle of the week—they came back, my mother and that man. Miss Burt had gotten me dressed to kill—shower, powder, tie, and the rest of it—and off we went, the three of us, to the judge's offices, next to a courtroom.

They were already married. Mr. Lyons said he was going to adopt me and I did not know what that meant. The judge was a kindly white-haired man, maybe sixty-five, with silver eyeglasses and a silver pocket watch that he took out two or three times. After a little friendly chatter, he came right to the point. "Do you know this man?" he asked.

I admitted that I had sort of gone fishing with him once.

Did I like him?

I looked at Mr. Lyons carefully. To tell the truth, he did not look all that familiar to me. "He's all right," I said.

"He's your father now, son, and he wants to adopt you."

I knew my mother had married this man but I was not quite sure where that put me. And I was still not sure that I would get out of the Burt School for good unless I kept my wits about me, which had never been a strong point. My pal could be wrong. Anybody could be wrong. Nothing, ever, was sure as stone. And my mother was keeping awfully quiet.

"If he's already my father," I said—the word sounded weird when it came out—"why does he have to a-dapt me?"

"A-dopt," the judge said, and then he began to explain to me all sorts of things about being adopted, some of which sounded all right, some of which I didn't understand. He'd explain something very slowly, then ask if I had understood him. I always nodded that I had. I didn't want to seem dumb as a slug. But I barely understood a word of it. My head buzzed. Those chest pains were beginning to kill me again. All I remember is that my name would have to be changed.

I looked at my mother. To tell the truth, she didn't look that familiar to me, either. She looked very pretty, though, in her polka-dot dress and wide-brimmed hat, with her soft brown curls. Would her name be changed, too? Yes. It had already been changed. A lot had been going on behind my back, like always. This name-changing business was unnerving. It was like becoming someone else entirely when I was not at all sure who I was already. I was Nathan Ress but everyone at school and at the Laurel House called me Nicki. I had rather gotten used to Nicki Ress. It rather went with me. So I said, if they didn't mind, I'd rather they did not change it, or that I even not get adapted, if I had anything to say about it all.

"You're being very silly," said Mr. Lyons. "Your mother has changed her name but *she* hasn't changed. She'll still be your mother and now I'm your father and—"

"I like my name the way it is," I said quietly.

"Don't be a child," Mr. Lyons said—a bit gruffly, I thought. "It's just your last name, and we can keep Ress as your middle name."

"It's all right, darling," said my mother, coming up close and putting her arm around me. Was she still my mother? She seemed more his, Mr. Lyons's, than mine. I was not sure who she was and I flinched when she touched me.

"I'd rather the boy decide for himself," the judge said firmly. "It's his decision, you know, folks."

"The kid's only eight," said Mr. Lyons, laughing lightly and shaking his head.

"Sometimes that has to be old enough. And I'd like to hear what he has to say, please."

"Take your time, Nicki," said my mother, smiling a little.

"Sure," said Mr. Lyons. "Take your time."

They all looked at me. I did not, at first, look at any of them. I looked at all of the framed documents on the judge's wall. I looked at my mother in her polka-dot dress; and she looked away. I looked closely, out of the corner of my eye, at Mr. Lyons. He was watching me carefully, with a friendly smile on his face.

"No hurry, Nicki," said the judge. "It's a big decision."

But there was a hurry. I could feel it pounding in my chest, anxious to be out. I thought my chest would break. It was tight as a drum and twisting madly. If I did not change my name, would they send me back? Anything could happen. There was surely only one thing to do. Surely my mother wanted me to agree. I could not take a chance of going back to that mausoleum. Anyway, not everyone gets a chance to choose his father and also his name.

We moved to a pretty little house with fake-stone siding in Mount Vernon, and I had a newly wallpapered room all to myself and a brand-new Schwinn two-wheeler and I sat down to breakfast and dinner with my mother and my new father and sometimes we went places together. And there was a Ping-Pong table in the basement and a garden framed by rosebushes in the backyard and I tried to figure out how I was supposed to act in this new arrangement. But within six months, a cold, wary center had begun to grow in me toward them. I did not like being told not to say "my" mother or "my" real father, and I couldn't get "Dad" or "Pop" or "Father" out of my mouth, which got to him too, which was reasonable, so the cold center grew and kept growing for decades until it turned to something worse.

2

DETACHMENT

Many years later, after a fitfully acquired degree from Penn, I served with the American Army at a small post in western France. It was a muddy installation, an enclave of Quonset huts and jerry-built tarpaper shacks and wooden supply sheds, of various lengths but otherwise indistinguishable. They had no names on them, no defining marks, so it was common to enter the wrong building. They were dreary, low structures, covered in tarpaper, each heated by a cast-iron potbellied stove that burned a gravelly coal and from which, every day or so, we had to remove and clean the bricks. The windows of dirty glass were sometimes covered with an opaque plastic sheet, to keep out the cold. In wet, warm weather, slugs ascended through the floorboards. The skies were always as gray and listless as the buildings and you never felt that the ground you walked upon was level and firm. On windy nights you went to sleep hearing the flag-pole cables knocking and the flapping of plastic against glass. The post was in the middle of a large flat, unprotected by hills or trees, and the wind could be sharp or, in the summer, thick with dust. There were few days without wind.

We were a medical detachment, though most of the men there were engineers sent to prepare for a hospital that, allegedly, might someday be built for a purpose no one could tell. Other than the engineers, who had little enough to do since no permanent structure had been started, there were administrators of various stripes, who administered the post without a clear function but were always busy, from warrant officers and a few captains and a colonel on down to me, at first a clerk typist. We were all there to support the engineers, who as yet had nothing to build. Only three times during the thirteen months I spent at Croix-Chapeau was the word "hospital" mentioned. No one knew for sure if it or any other building would ever be built. No one ever talked about the future of the post. It was *just there*, as if it had been there in the mud for years, and it looked for all its impermanence as if it would be there long after I left, as long as those tarpaper shacks could withstand the rain and wind. No one knew why the place was called "Croix-Chapeau."

This was in the early 1950s and there were already demonstrations by the local citizens in nearby La Rochelle against the remaining American troops, who weren't there to occupy France but for some other reason that someone, somewhere, thought fit. It was one thing to save a proud country, another to hang around breeding discontent—for a couple of years, then five, and by the time I left a full ten years after the war had ended. Stone and stucco walls in the town had "Go Home Américain" painted on them in large, dripping red letters. There was a riot in March and several machine guns were mounted on the parapets of American headquarters in La Rochelle but no shots were fired, either way, despite a lot of cursing and flag-waving and raised fists. Nothing happened close to Croix-Chapeau; I don't think anyone cared much about the place except for the few French who lived nearby and could make some money from the situation.

This was the first time I had experienced such hate toward America. At first it shocked me, though it was soon clear why the French despised Americans, beyond their mannerisms and coarse sounds and indifference to all that was French. There were reported rapes. Once I saw a couple of guys from the post run down an elderly Frenchman on a bicycle and steal the familiar baguette attached to the back of his bike, and then run off, shouting something with the word "frog" in it; others sprayed bikers with fire extinguishers and laughed wildly.

"The frogs would be talking kraut if we hadn't come," Bill Baldini, the short, stocky, red-faced second baseman, told me with authority, "and now they tell us to go home. Well, fuck them. Fuck every last one of them frogs." Why, he speculated, couldn't all the French be like the docile women, for some reason called "P-ladies," who came to the post fence every evening at dusk to pick up and deliver our laundry? They smiled, they were as reliable as a Swiss clock, and they liked us and liked the francs that were just so much scrap paper to us.

Demi Maneri, a short intense man who practically had epileptic fits when he was riled, coached all of the sports teams on the post. He was within months of rotating back to the States when I arrived in January, during the basketball season. He checked the personnel records of everyone coming to Croix-Chapeau, and since I had played basketball for the University of Pennsylvania he promptly had me transferred out of the office pool, where I typed and filed, and into a job as his assistant. The basketball season was winding down and the team, with its six men, hadn't yet won a game. Then, because of a scheduling problem, we played three games in two days in a cold field hangar, and I managed to score a slew of points, and we won all three. So he made me coach for the last three games, two of which we won, and then, when he rotated back to the States in March, I was put in charge of the entire sports program, his job, and spent the next year in that capacity, coaching all of the post teams, even baseball, which I had only played in its softball incarnation, and even catching, after we lost two catchers, one to rotation, the other to a statutory rape charge involving a fifteen-year-old girl from Bordeaux. I caught three games, adequately, nabbed two runners trying to steal second, went zero for nineteen at bat, then leaped for a riser with my bare right hand and had the bone in my ring finger pop through the skin. The company doctor jerked it back into its proper position and applied a band-aid. This ended my baseball days. That finger never knit properly and often locks rigid when I dig into my pocket for change, more than sixty-five years later.

NEARLY EVERYONE HATED the dog called Guilty. Dogs ran in packs at the base and there were a lot of them, perhaps fifteen or twenty, mostly mutts, all running free within the fenced grounds of the 22nd Medical Detachment at Croix-Chapeau, foraging as they could, attaching themselves to one or another of the soldiers, all of whom took keen pleasure in tormenting Guilty. They threw stones at him, shouted, *"Allez,* Guilty!" while pointing a finger at the dog, and then laughed wildly and kept pointing when the mutt put down his head and slouched away. Sometimes they'd beckon the poor creature close, offer him a bone or some gristle, and then snatch the food away, cackling. Guilty never learned. They did their worst, threw a stone or heavy stick at him, and the dog would merely put out his tongue and seem to smile, as if this were a game he liked or at least the source of some attention. The dogs hated Guilty too, and rarely allowed him into their pack, never near food that had been thrown to them. They bared their teeth, made low growling noises, and he smiled back or skulked away, turning both cheeks. When they were copulating—always a spectacle that drew crowds at Croix-Chapeau—Guilty lay at a distance with his head against the ground, breathing heavily, drooling, as he often did. Since no one had more than a few hours of work to do each day, most of the troops liked to stand around in groups whenever possible, harassing Guilty. It was one of the main sports at that isolated post.

As director of sports at such a small installation with no facilities, I had much practical work to attend to. I asked the engineers, who had nothing to do, to clear and level a field, lay out a baseball diamond, build several rows of stands, a kind of makeshift dugout, and a wooden fence to contain the outfield. The result was better than I expected. When they heard that I liked to punch the speed bag and could do so with some skill, they built a firm platform for me and, barehanded, I banged the bag for hours, forgetting about the books I had begun to devour and the chatter of my fellow troops, until the knuckles on both hands bled and my arms were too tired to lift. I was bored and frustrated and I did not have the faintest idea what I wanted to do with my life except that I knew it would not be related to the life I had lived before I'd volunteered for the Army. I hit the bag with anger and some skill, and Dan Tedrick, a UPI reporter who wrote for *Stars and Stripes*, got a cartoonist to draw a funny image of me at it and wrote a short piece about how I could play "Yankee Doodle" on the bag, which was a stretch.

When I arrived at Croix-Chapeau from Fort Knox, the ungraded earth between the Quonset huts and shacks was runneled with brown snow, and you could not help stepping in it; and it was always dark, cold, gray, and drizzling, with a kind of pervasive gray and wetness that crept inside you, kept you always rubbing your arms or hugging yourself. I rolled down the thin mattress on the wire springs of my bunk that first day and threw my duffel on it. From Fort Knox I had traveled by train to a troopship which had taken us to Bremerhaven; and then we'd gone by train to Paris, my first glimpse of Paris, and during the six-hour layover from midnight until early the next morning I had walked from the Gare du Nord to the Place de la Madeleine, then up to Montmartre and back. My head was flooded with images of Paris and I could not sleep on the train to La Rochelle. A brown Army bus took us to Croix-Chapeau and in the early afternoon I collapsed and slept.

A sign on the wall of my tarpaper shack announced that pissing from the windows was not permitted. The footlocker at the end of the bed next to mine was open and filled with five six-packs of German beer. A metal closet opposite my little area in the drab room was open too, and I could see a rough-edged tear sheet pasted there, with the image of a naked woman, her legs spread, with a guy's head several inches below the V, facing up. The bed, the footlocker, and the metal closet belonged to a fellow named Homer A. Moose and whenever there was a general inspection of the post, one of the officers loaded Moose and all of his goods onto a deuce-and-a-half truck and drove him through the countryside for the time the inspectors poked here and there.

AT FIRST THE dogs annoyed me. They were like emboldened furies. They had the run of the post and there were so many of them and they were always chasing one another, or badgering you, looking for food. Guilty—part terrier, with a little poodle thrown in, a mongrel mostly spotted dark gray and silver gray, flecked with black—was distinguished by nothing greater than the enthusiasm he always showed, and those actions that had caused him to be so named. The soldiers in their loathing for the creature thought up as many ways as possible to humiliate him. There was a small police dog named Lady that they had taught to hate black men; Lady was often kept near the financial office, which issued paychecks, and when black soldiers came to the pay window, Lady would growl and bark and bare her teeth, and they'd grab their envelopes and vanish, amid catcalls from the whites and the Puerto Ricans. When Lady went into heat, they brought her into the orderly room and summoned Guilty, who was ecstatic about his prospects. But they knew Lady would not have the mutt, and though Guilty chased her around the room vigorously he never got to her; everyone had a good laugh, and then they summarily kicked the mutt, herding it outside, into the pack of manic dogs that had been leaping up at the windows and scratching the door.

Gays were recycled off the post; Puerto Ricans were there in sufficient numbers not to be harassed and they blended in with the whites; but the black soldiers got it from all angles at Croix-Chapeau. Clyde Bowen, a great junk-ball pitcher, a small man, older than most of the troops, ebony and very silent, often had four or five guys raise a fist to their mouths when he came to bat or pitched, pretending to be shooting a blow dart.

I speculated that Guilty might be the reincarnation of Franz Kafka, whom I had started to read, and with whom I had begun to identify; I knew he was surely guilty irrespective of any sin. I have never kept a dog or had an attachment to one, and only because Guilty might have appreciated that I didn't harass him may have led the dog to slouch around my sports shack, tongue out, needy, altogether avid for some good word. I gave the dog little encouragement but never pointed, never raised my voice. A new friend, Sandy, adopted the dog quite seriously. Sandy was from New York and had a degree in history, so we got to talking and I was pleased to have Guilty off my hands. He hadn't been much of a pal for me, and though Sandy and I became friends, I was desperate in that bleak place for another kind of companionship, which I eventually found in a seedy bar on the outskirts of Rochefort.

My job took only a few hours a day and since I was providing recreation for my fellow troops, they generally liked me, at least were pleasant enough to me, and I often went to the back of my small tarpaper shack in the early afternoon and read one of the small books I had bought or found. I was tentatively mad for books. In my teens, fishing and basketball, as well as mountains of ambiguity and tension, defined me. I had the mumps for several months before I joined the Army and as I lay in bed, my balls the size of baseballs, I tried several books but could not concentrate. I knew that I was missing a bundle of somethings, but didn't know what. I had a degree in economics from the Wharton School but I had rarely read anything I had not been assigned to read in school and felt starved for some vague meal that, somehow, might include books.

In a rummage sale near Fort Knox I had found a battered Portable Hemingway, with a faded red cloth cover. I bought it for a quarter, only because it fit so neatly into one of the top pockets of my olive drab field jacket. I had loitered with the book on a scorching June afternoon there in Louisville, randomly flipping pages, reading the terse vignettes from *In Our Time* that were interlaced between the stories, thinking that I had never read prose so crisp and athletic. Like the best basketball players I knew, the writing was tight and economical—and it accelerated with electric speed and surprise. I started one story that began, "The train went on up the track and out of sight," and then showed me a town that was no longer a town but a burnt remnant, and a deep river swirling against the log spiles of the bridge on which the young man stood, watching the trout holding themselves, facing upstream—as I knew trout did—in the faster water.

When I finished reading "Big Two-Hearted River," I winced. It was so close to my own days along rivers, and I promptly read it through again, fast, and then yet again, very slowly. I was Nick Lyons and I was Nick in the story. I had looked down from such bridges hundreds of times, I understood such water and had caught such trout; and I had held the fragments of my life together, like the other Nick, by returning to that thing I loved so privately and passionately. I had not known that writing about trout fishing, about hooks and lines and grasshoppers and rivers—or any writing, on any subject whatsoever—could be so intimate, so visceral.

I had been so stunned by the simple revelation that this could be that thing called literature, something that could haul me into its world and wake every part of me, that I did not feel, for an hour afterward, the pain on the skin above my right ankle. The strip of flesh between my pants cuff and sock was bright red, blistered sorely from the Kentucky sun. I had been so absorbed that I'd noticed nothing. Then, back in this world, my lower leg felt as if someone had run a rasp across it, very hard. It seemed like a symbol of something.

AND SO, SOMEHOW, a fire had been lit inside me, and I craved reading, as one book led to another, and one by an author that touched me led to three others by the same author. On a furlough from Fort Knox a friend gave me Kafka's stories and I plunged, stunned again, into that haunting world of Kafka— only the first serious author I read after Hemingway. I read randomly, compulsively—a smörgåsbord of the slick, the silly, and the profoundly serious—Steinbeck and Jack London, Spillane, Patrick Dennis, Salinger, Poe—anything I could find that would fit into one of the top pockets of my field jacket. Sometime that fall I had made an irrevocable decision not to go into the insurance brokerage business, for which my stepfather had married my mother, in the late years of the Depression, and I began, for the first time in my life, to read as food for some deep and inchoate hunger. Where it would lead, I didn't know. How much intellectual capacity I had for navigating such deep waters, with so many conflicting currents, was a total mystery to me. I was adrift but paddling for my life in a dozen directions at once. Where was I headed? How could I possibly earn a living now that I had abandoned the only field I had been trained to enter?

Could I write? At the PX there were typewriters you could use by inserting a quarter for a fifteen-minute block. I did put in the quarter, type a few words about some fishing trip, then stare at the white paper, and eventually pound the keys crazily. Writing was hopeless.

The Army, I now see, beyond the boredom, the emptiness, the savagery, was a buffer zone, a time without consequences, a dangling couple of years when I could work through some of these matters and not have to worry about what the world or my parents or any other soul in the universe thought. What became the all-consuming obsession of my life in Croix-Chapeau, what must have made me seem pretentious in the extreme, and self-important, was my total preoccupation with myself, with the conceit that I could find out who I was and where I could go, and even find a road map there, in a book, even in this bleak outpost, overrun with mongrel dogs, a place without purpose or future, detached from all else, from almost everyone.

THERE WAS A lot of talk about religion and sex at Croix-Chapeau; they were the two main topics. Gonzalez, a Catholic, thought Stevenson, an agnostic, was surely damned, and Stevenson argued that it was probably a greater sin to stiff the whores in Rochefort, which Gonzalez regularly did. Someone brought a whore back in a bus from La Rochelle, a hard girl in a light blue silky dress, and she provided service with hand and mouth to a dozen American troops on the short trip. Did the colonel's wife really have sex with animals, as George Lowes reported? Did the women who came to the fence to take and drop off our laundry want to increase their take-home pay? Had Joe Devona really screwed McKenzie's nineteen-year-old wife a week after she gave birth to their daughter? Two guys reported that they'd seen the blood, and had seen the girl begging to see Devona. In a world in which there was no shooting, no combat, no purpose for being where we were, such arguments and speculations and stories were rampant.

For myself, I argued not at all—and for a while I was quietly obsessed with Jeanne, a prostitute in the bar on the outskirts of Rochefort, a tall blonde with the features of a farm girl who was old enough to have slept with Nazis. I'd had little experience with the flesh—and I was shy of it. The closest I got to hard-core sex in my teens came on warm wet nights when for fishing I collected those big worms, nightcrawlers, hermaphrodites, joined at the collar. I knew any successes might lead to reactions I couldn't avoid, and a lot of my future freedom might be jeopardized, so I never jeopardized it. Touching and a lot of clumsy persuasion that persuaded not at all and was more than faintly dishonest. Kissing. Hands and body shifting, flinching, silently shouting, to protect. Not much fun in any of it and since I was of no mind to be serious, had not the faintest idea who I would be the next day, it was all, always, a failed enterprise. Then about the time I found the Louvre, I tried a hooker on the Rue de Rivoli and it all seemed safe, quick, and uninvolved, though there was less there than had met the eye. Jeanne wasn't quite as quick and seemed safe to my untrained eye. She was really quite fetching—five-nine or -ten, thin, with modest breasts and lemon-yellow hair that tumbled a foot from her head, always in slight disorder. She would not have been out of place as a model in a small city, or a librarian, or a lawyer's wife. She appeared to enjoy her work well enough and had none of her older sister's brash grating voice; nor did she do any of the sex tricks in public with broomsticks and coins by which her sister made extra francs. My interest in the little bar centered only on Jeanne, so for a while I could be called monogamous. Even when I went to Paris after that, which I did more and more, I avoided the women.

In Paris, the Winged Victory sent shivers through me when I first saw it at the Louvre, and so did Mantegna's St. Sebastian, wounded, pierced by so many arrows, his eyes skyward, I began to have feelings, sensations, I'd never had before. I felt the breadth and scope of Delacroix, with fifty or sixty figures all part of the great orchestral sound; and the riveting intensity of Rembrandt's single-image slaughtered and hung-up ox, its flesh bright tawny red and gold. But Chardin's *The Ray* affected me most—the broad flat fish trussed up, hung up to drain, glowering, with entrails and oysters there too, and the knife that had done the work half-buried, while the hunched cat looked on—quiet, patient, ferocious.

I saw my first Van Gogh on one trip, possibly in the Jeu de Paume, and felt the powerful surge of his compressed tension, the agitated lines, the petals of the flower imbued with a flame that came from gut and heart. I had never experienced anything like the Van Gogh, the Chardin, the Rembrandt. Books twisted my gut perhaps, confusing me with what I did not yet know and had to know, numbing my chest, sending my head into a spin; none of it was as visceral as these paintings, the first paintings I'd looked at with any care.

The city itself assaulted me, and whenever I was outside I walked: from the great flea market in Montmartre, into Pigalle, up and down both sides of the Seine, into Montparnasse. It was aimless but determined walking mostly—walking that tried to find paths in the maze, meanings in what was charged with meanings I could not decipher. I wanted to see and remember all the details, devour the city. And as I walked my early years flooded back—in Mount Vernon, then Brooklyn, and the years at Penn—all of it trifling beside Notre-Dame, inconsequential in the museums. And Paris washed through me as I walked, like water in a pan, leaving specks of gold, hints of what might be built from the near wreck I'd made of my life.

When I first ascended to the soft job of managing the little sports program, I inherited Demi's blunt tarpaper shack for myself and another building in which all the sneakers and uniforms were kept. Sandy couldn't take the raucous chatter of the troops and more raucous radio music late at night, and every night I would lock him in the storage building with Guilty. My space was grungy and small but it was well lit and there was a desk and a bed and a chair. I found an old Underwood Standard typewriter in the typing pool, cleaned and oiled it and got a new ribbon and for want of any stories to write began a journal. I typed separate sheets of paper and planned eventually to bind them with the roll of cloth tape I found in the storage shack, used to tape ankle sprains. The journal was all I could dredge up about Nick, emotional, social, sexual. The break in the continuum of my so-called life had cut loose a torrent of recollections, a hunt for the causes of my malaise. Years of report cards that continued to announce, "Could do better." All those dead-quiet dinners at home and the increasing coldness to my mother and stepfather, Arthur. A growing love of basketball—practicing dribbling in our dark garage in Brooklyn, tapping the ball against a wall with my left hand, willing ambidextrous skills, jumping rope by the hour so I could levitate on the court. Reading nothing, ever, but what was assigned. Hungering for some girlfriend among the tempting, guarded girls of Brooklyn in the 1940s, one who invited me to touch her after she heard that my touch would not make her pregnant. Avoiding the kiss, the hug, the touch of Arthur or my mother. An escape into the textured world of fishing, finding some minor satisfactions in learning to tie a knot that held, a fly that floated, a world with a thousand chances for temporal successes, the compelling suspense, enough failures to teach that I could survive failures of a lost fish, a bumbled cast, and more. Failure to make the high school basketball team—the worst in the city—twice. The only one of thirty-five students to be cashiered from a popular writing course. Failure always to be more than an awkward grabber with Susan or Marjorie, the sources of damp dreams. My pal Ira and I built an igloo every winter in the backyard of my parents' home and in it talked sports seriously, and careers, hating all options for the latter. My friend Mort and I took exhausting trips by subway and train to fish overcrowded rivers eighty miles from Brooklyn, our only days in nature. Bike rides to Steeplechase Pier at Coney Island to haul hackleheads and an occasional flatfish up thirty feet. Nothing prompted me, as I wrote the pages of the journal, to be worth more than these pages that came to so little, that I would want no one to read. All those years, as exciting as stone. And always, somehow, wherever I was and whatever I did, I leaned like a magnet to the numinous world of water, hungry for the mystery beneath the surface, the electric jolt when a fish takes the bait, a bobber dips under, the line tugs.

Sitting at that well-oiled typewriter, I found nothing in the Brooklyn I knew that was worth a story, a poem. Lenny may have made it with his sister, Warren pounded nails into doorbell buttons on Halloween, someone lit a fire of leaves beneath a car the same night—and it never seemed to me a Brooklyn with even the fleshy stories much later found in Henry Roth. But I was always restless and saw too little beyond my navel.

I must have wanted to write even then, or at least have a quiet place of my own, because when I was in my early teens I fashioned a little office for myself in the basement of our house in Brooklyn. We had heated the place with coal, which had been delivered through a fouled window into a coal bin, and which I'd shoveled into the furnace. When my stepfather switched to oil, the coal bin was left empty. I scrubbed off the soot for a week and papered the walls with fishing scenes from *Field & Stream* and *Outdoor Life*. The area was lit by a single hanging bulb. I used a twelve-inch board, attached to both sides of the bin, for a desk and for more than a year I went to it frequently—though there's no evidence I wrote a word, certainly none that I kept.

BUT IN MY tarpaper office with my head full of words and art, I began to loathe the abject wastefulness of most of my days, organizing the baseball team, accounting for all of the sports equipment—T-shirts, shorts, baseball and basketball uniforms, several sets of sneakers, cleats. It's always a pleasure to see a good athlete move and we had several: Tom White, a

Minnesotan who had played minor-league ball and was an amazing shortstop; Dave Billinger, the pitcher with a superb riser, and Bill Long, a fastballer; and Tommy "Talking" Tengan at second, after Bill Baldini recycled. The chatter of baseball has its compelling rhythms, its own happy jargon. And we laughed a lot and I tried to make the nine players into a coherent team. But I could feel myself drifting away from the world of sport, which had sustained me during my teens, during my college years. Baseball talk was not what I wanted to hear, the games became more and more distant, and the chatter of the players went through me like barbed wire.

So I shut out the sounds and retreated to my little shack and made busywork for myself with the supplies. A large crate of cheap tennis sneakers came in one day and I could not imagine what they were for, and over the next eight months I simply gave them outright to anyone who might use a pair. Accounting for these and other equipment—mostly of the cheapest kind, bought wholesale at a bargain—was a nightmare, and whenever possible I punched the speed bag or read another book rather than work out the details of such a shipment. Every minute away from books, away from the journal I'd begun to keep religiously, scraping words from my brain, all the dirt and ugliness unleavened by any joy, every minute with the baseball team or the engineers made me tense and irritable.

From Hemingway I became interested in bullfights and went to Zaragoza, then Madrid, where I saw the great Ordóñez one afternoon, radiant in the midst of the pageantry, the bright sound of the trumpets, the drama of life and death. In Madrid, as in Paris, I sought this new world of museums, which I had just discovered, and was mesmerized by the Goyas, the

Rembrandts, the miraculous Velázquez portraits. There was so much to see and learn.

Outside of the drama inside me, the world went on as before or changed abruptly. Dan Tedrick went to Bordeaux to hear Billy Graham and came back solidly born again. Duffy, our second-string third baseman, rode his motorcycle off the road on his way to practice one day and was decapitated. There was another general inspection and they again loaded Moose onto a truck, along with his footlocker and metal closet, and drove him around for three hours. Pop Fernandez couldn't beat a statutory rape charge and I became catcher on the baseball team for a few weeks. I found reasons to drive to Paris every chance I got. Gary Schumacher, a jewelry maker who traded currency, introduced me to Raymond Duncan, and the old fellow, in toga and sandals, told me that if I wanted to write I ought to do so letter by letter, like he did, composing directly onto his typesetting board, so each letter would have its special meaning. He seemed like a silly old fart to me and I was never curious enough to read a word he had typeset.

I thought hard about taking my discharge in Paris and living there; I had never loved a city with such passion and I still knew it only slenderly. And I thought wildly that I might become a mercenary in Israel or join the French Foreign Legion. But in the end, I caught some glimpse of my colossal ignorance and realized that I had to make my stand with English, in America.

MANY YEARS LATER, I met my old friend Sandy for lunch. Our lives had taken vastly different routes and in time had been defined by what we had done, how we had lived, and we talked first of some of those matters and then, tentatively, sank into the sweet swamp of nostalgia, recalling the details of Croix-Chapeau building by building, and a dozen of the main players in that short drama, even the dog Guilty, his pal. He told me how the pitcher Hastings, drunk on the mound, had once keeled over in the middle of a game and just lay there laughing. He told me of a report that had been filed after Homer A. Moose had been caught throwing a brick through a French store window, the case called "The Apprehension of Moose." He told me that our friend Jack Carmichael, who always drove wildly in France and had a trick of steering with his elbows and turning full-face to someone in the back seat, had died in a car accident on the West Side Highway soon after he returned to the States; he told me that after he had taken a brief furlough and returned to the post he had learned that someone—he never found out who—had decapitated Guilty. He mentioned some of our games of baseball and basketball and I produced for his inspection my still-locking finger. He said that Jeanne had asked after me several times and I told him about my trip back on the troopship, guarding a kid slated for the stockade who had "Hate" and "Love" tattooed for all time on the his knuckles and threatened to give me one or the other if I harassed him while we were cleaning brooms off the bow, by tying them onto ropes and tossing them into the wake—though he tossed some in without the benefit of rope.

It was trivial old stuff, most of it, and it had taken place a great while earlier. But later, on my long walk uptown, alone, my head swarmed with images of Croix-Chapeau and what, if anything, that year might have meant. By that December I had been desperate to rotate back to the States and begin some new life that nibbled at my brain. On the last afternoon, before the bus left for La Rochelle, when the warrant officer abruptly told me to return all of the better sneakers I had been issued for the various programs, I just threw my hands up. Sneakers! I was obsessed with the fate of Joseph K. and making the troopship that would leave Bremerhaven the next day, and those high-sided Converse basketball sneakers were irrelevant, idiotic, scattered; they had been worn for a full season or two. It would take me a week to collect them and I could not possibly get them all—some had in fact gone back to America with the players who had worn them. They were gone, worn, useless, and some of the then-current basketball team needed what was left, as soon as the next night. I should simply have told the mealy old careerist, but did not for a minute want to miss that bus. So I delivered a box to his door with nineteen pairs of those cheap tennis sneakers and marked the case closed, made the bus, took the train to Bremerhaven, and was on the troopship for six days, in a stormy North Atlantic crossing.

By the time I got to Fort Dix, where I was holding before discharge, I had forgotten about the sneakers. But the warrant officer had phoned ahead. He had passionately insisted that I be court-martialed at once for theft of Army property. The captain who interviewed me on the subject did not want to search my bags for the errant equipment, nor hear my explanation, nor send me back in irons to Croix-Chapeau. He shook his head, smiled slightly, and let me slip quietly into the tumultuous forest of New York City, full of possibility and alligators.

I had not thought for all these years of Jeanne, who had given me my faint first taste of what then passed for affection, and I thought of my last brief visit to that grubby hangout near Rochefort. She had been sick—coughing, weak, thinner, perhaps with something unalterably bad—and I had merely shaken her hand. I thought of the monstrous violence in Guilty's fate and the mud and the idiocy. And then I began to close off that odd year or so, so many years earlier, that hinge, that empty time so full of meaning, that ugly place full of false starts and illusions and violence and genuine seeds, and I tried to see the young man I had been before, playing basketball with such abandon, desperate to find any scrubby path out of the swamp in which I found myself. I had not yet felt the full power and force of my ignorance.

3

A VERY SMALL ROOM

When I returned, I moved into a snot-green room on West Tenth Street in Greenwich Village. The room—once a walk-in closet or a john—was exactly four and a half strides long. The bed wedged sideways into two snug alcoves at the far end; there was a sink whose porcelain had been chewed in a dozen places by rust; there was a hot plate, a narrow metal desk, a distressed chair. On one of the dirty walls a previous tenant had hung a Christ with a crown of thorns, ripped from a newsprint magazine and put carelessly into a Woolworth frame. The half window over the bed opened onto the back alleyway of a posh restaurant, and on warm spring nights I could hear the clanking and clinking of dishes and silverware, smell a dozen amiable mixed scents, and hear occasional high laughter. Somehow it was now time to wrench my life, by violence if necessary, from that old path into one I had only glimpsed in France. I had not a shred of evidence that I could change, simply a blind, bulldog belief or hope that there was nothing else for me and that if I did not change, or could not, I might see fit to do real violence to myself. This very small room, the barest base, was where I must make my stand. The rent was eight dollars per week; I could stay here forever.

After the slightest raised voice from my stepfather, I left the house in Brooklyn the day after my discharge from the Army. I took the subway to the Village, walked for half a dozen blocks with my Army duffel bag slung over one shoulder, carrying the portable typewriter I had used since high school, and even a fishing rod, and, when I saw a "Room for Rent" sign, found what I was searching for. After I had laid out the few clothes I had taken, the half dozen books I could carry, some paper and pens, I walked into the maze of streets and did not return until well after midnight. I took those nocturnal walks for five months, nearly every night, often until the sky grew lighter, and then returned to my tiny room, my world, and lay on the cot, exhausted, unable to sleep, my head a hive of fragmented memories and false starts, listening to a strange gnashing sound from a neighbor on the other side of my wall, grinding his teeth together for hours in the night, like some small animal inside the walls, trying to claw and chew its way into the light.

Haphazardly, passionately, by a kind of dumb survival instinct, I continued my slide into the vast wilderness of books, that jungle where paths can go on forever or lead to some great swamp. And I felt again and again that itch to write—but what? I sat at the old metal desk for ten, twelve hours a day, sometimes standing to pace like a caged leopard in that small room, often with a book in hand. I wrote mawkish poems that jingled and clanked, stories that never began, rarely ended, without arc or point. The stories had one dull character in common; he was always there—perhaps with a twisted nose or hair of a different color or texture, or only three fingers on his left hand, but he had a degree from the Wharton School or some other business college and had been in the Army, he hated his stepfather, loved basketball and fishing, and was unmistakably, undeniably, a very dead ringer for me.

I felt a brave new freedom. I knew no one and had to speak to no one, and I spoke only when spoken to; I could drink anything, anywhere, and rearrange the day and night to suit my fancy; I could write until my fingers were heavy as lead or read until my eyes drooped; I could dress any way I wanted, comb or not comb my long curly hair, walk anywhere, read whatever I chose. The comforting order, which I had hated and loved, was gone. I found the caged basketball courts on Sixth Avenue near Fourth Street and joined in those savage pickup games, full court, with hard street kids who played at a fierce and fast and brilliant level. I could still play decent ball but the games were less and less important to me and they left me too exhausted, especially after I went back to school.

After a month of rampant freedom, I knew I needed a road map, some semblance of structure, or I'd slip into right field, and my solution was to register for four courses at the nearby New School—a poetry workshop, one on short story writing, another on playwriting; I vaguely hoped someone would see a spark of talent in one of those. The last was called English Prose Style and today, so many years later, it is the only one I can remember. I had thought it would be a how-to-do-it, like the pedestrian writing courses I took and soon found worth-less. It was not. It was taught by a man not much older than me, Keith Botsford, and to me, at that time, he was electrify-ing. He would come into the grungy classroom only partly filled with night-school students of various stripes—shabby would-be writers slumped in boredom, dropouts, businessmen wanting to improve themselves, a fading beauty with her stun-ning daughter—never with a note or notebook or handout, and sit cross-legged on the desk, always with a Coke, which he would open soon after he arrived and sip slowly while he talked. He often dressed like a Wall Street broker but with a touch or two that said the elegant clothes were merely a uniform; the bright vest, sparkling shoes, handkerchief in breast pocket or carnation in his lapel confirmed that he was really not of that world but—to use a word he frequently spoke with approba-tion—a dandy. He announced that he had been quadrilingual from birth and frequently sprinkled in perfectly pronounced phrases in French, German, or Italian. He didn't lecture; he talked. Often he talked for the entire three hours, looking rather aristocratic in his dark silky way, about philosophy, poetry, architecture, art, archeology, all manner of fiction, and six-teenth- to twentieth-century prose in its many incarnations, our primary subject. He talked and talked, regularly without pausing for more than a brief query to our odd class, about some matter in a book we were supposed to have read. Either no one responded or his question had been merely rhetorical, for finally no one spoke in his class.

He assigned eight hundred to a thousand pages of reading each week—Bishop Hugh Latimer, Thomas Nashe, John Lyly, Sir Thomas More, Lodge, Hooker, Dekker, Sir Thomas Browne, Milton, Sterne, Jeremy Taylor, all of Jane Austen, four of the longest novels by Henry James. He was brash and seemed to know everyone and everything. I read every word he assigned: *The Garden of Cyrus, or The Quincunx Mystically Considered, Hydriotaphia, Religio Medici* in one of the early weeks of little sleep, remembering little except some of Browne's stunning phrases, electric moments. Somewhere in one of the books Botsford assigned, none of which I had heard of—and none included in the one English course I had taken at Penn—somewhere in one of them I hoped I would find an invitation to the Proper Path, a clear map to whatever it was I might be seeking, perhaps some faint hint as to what that might be, though I never did. Botsford seemed to know all three books by Browne by heart. He quoted liberally from them as he talked and never opened one of the texts. He did likewise with a dozen other texts.

I had run from my classes at Penn, playing pool and seeing movies late into the night, losing myself in basketball and pinochle, despairing of the world of literature after that one course with three hundred students, racing from Beowulf to Virginia Woolf. All I remembered from those days were the drama of Sol Huebner telling us that he had gone to Congress and insisted that they "put a dollar value on a human life" and a professor relating an anecdote to illustrate *caveat emptor* with a shopkeeper asking a farmer, "Hey, Joe, are dose tomats freze?" Now I could not study hard enough, reading with the sure thought that this was a meal for my brain, something I needed to live.

Reeling from the sounds of such prose, the rhythms and phrases, I wandered off on one of my nightly jaunts, more vigorously than before. I thought about a speed-reading course I had decided I needed to keep up with the reading, and about the woman, aged thirty or so, who taught it. After two sessions she told me emphatically that though I had made a little progress with speed and comprehension, she assured me with authority that I was too late to the dance. "Saints with powers of levitation," she said, "couldn't rise from the hole you've dug."

When I soon realized that I needed not to read faster but much more slowly, I quit the course.

I walked up to Central Park and then back downtown by another route; I went to the old Fulton Fish Market, alive at three in the morning with sounds and smells and motion, and marveled at the bluefish, stripers, salmon, and cod, so much larger than any fish I had caught, and all the while phrases from Browne, "Life is a pure flame," "The world that I regard is myself," "The huntsmen are up in America," rocketed in my brain, and then, trying to find my own words for the details of the city I had just seen, or remembering a phrase from Nashe or Lyly, I started at a half run, anxious to be back in my little room, as night gave way to the first faint light of day, so I could think not about plots or theories but about the way these people wrote, the immeasurable possibilities of language—not merely new words but how they were put together, how in their bones and muscle and syntax they were stunning, rewiring my brain.

At first I had tried to write six or seven hours a day, in a rush, to fill that vague but gnawing hunger in my heart. There was a coiled heat in me, beating on a drum skin to get out. Soon, just as I had begun to read more slowly, I began to write with deliberation, and regularly, and to correct what I had done the day before rather than flee from it.

At the small metal desk I learned *Sitzfleisch*, sitting for long hours, trying to write something of worth, not for fame or glory or even money, but to quell that great hunger in my heart to be taken seriously. After I had begun to finish and submit dozens of poems and stories, and to send them out into the world like so many arrows, randomly shot, I would go every morning—first lingering in the dark hallway for a glimpse of Diane, the shy light-footed ballet dancer two doors away, who fled from me—to check the mailbox. My mailbox was always host to a steady stream of rejections. I recycled my miserable words and filled several shoeboxes with the emphatic, minimalist rejections. At first, these were printed notices to the effect that (a) the magazine received a huge number of submissions; (b) someone had in fact read what I had scraped off my brain; (c) what I had done was not—for some perfectly good but unnamed reason—their cup of tea. The *New Yorker* returned my submissions so fast that in the mad blur of those intense days in the mid-1950s I often thought that I had submitted a particular work the day before—or even that morning—and that they had a Special Agent of Rejection at the main post office. Though I had persuaded myself that I was not writing for fame or money, those curt slaps hurt. "What poems do you read?" Botsford asked me one night after class. The class had dwindled to five or six of us, and I may have been the last of those who sat riveted, trying to take in all the words that flowed those long hours, interspersed only by sips from the ubiquitous Coca-Cola bottle. I had mentioned that I was writing some poetry and he had quietly refused to look at it though I only hinted, never offered.

I told him "Invictus" was one of my favorites.

He looked at me for a moment and then roared: "'Invictus!'" He smiled and shook his head vigorously. "Oh good heavens, no. Not 'Invictus.'"

I looked away and lifted my shoulders.

He kept shaking his head and went on gaily: "My unconquerable soul. My bloody head. Master of my fate. You poor little booby. You poor soul. That's a dreadful, poem, Nicki—positively dreadful. Read Yeats and Donne and Hopkins and Leopardi and Rimbaud and Baudelaire and a thousand other poets before you ever read that dreadful, dreadful little poem again. Now I know what you need. Now I know precisely what you need. Do you know what that is, you lover of unbowed bloody heads?"

I shook my head.

"An education. Before you do anything else whatsoever, get yourself an education." And he hoisted the black cape he sometimes wore over his jacket, shook his head, and vanished.

As THE DAYS of spring wore on I kept repeating most of my old patterns. I paced my little room, my head remaining full of doubts; I walked at night until my legs were lead, etherized to the outside world, to my family, my affection increasingly cold, protective. Often, late on a rainy night, I lay on my cot and looked at the garish Christ with his wide, sad eyes and one tear balanced always on an underlid, who anyway was not my Christ; and often that same grinding of teeth came through the thin wall, which I had by now learned was from the mouth of a Hungarian seaman who had lost his girlfriend, his great love, and with her all of his substantial inheritance. I thought of choices, even lifelong choices, and I tried to measure whether as the several months had passed I had come any closer to where I vaguely imagined I wanted to be. Sometimes when I sat at my desk for hours without writing a word, I'd slam the keys with both hands. Then I'd try to read one of Botsford's assignments but throw the book down. And finally I'd race from the little room, suddenly a tomb, into the streets so full of faces and lights at any hour. In the Army I had been told when to eat, when to dress, when to sleep. I had total freedom now— to walk, brood, search for who knew what, at whatever hour it suited my fancy. One night I went to the Bowery and immediately felt part of the destitute and forlorn, a castoff or failure or bum; on another I crisscrossed the Village, looking hungrily into every face, tasting none of the great intellectual wine I had heard flowed here, speaking to no one, for what would I talk about, "Invictus"?

One night I was buffaloing along in my ratty Army field jacket—hirsute, my hair long and tousled—headed for Central Park, and I had reached the crowded theater district just north and west of Times Square. I paused for a moment to look at several of the billboards and heard a voice say, "Nicki?" and I turned and saw a man I was sure I had never met, his face unknown to me. He was dressed in a Brooks Brothers blue blazer, a button-down blue shirt, a striped tie, and his hair was plastered flat; a handsome well-dressed woman held his arm. "Is that Nicki Lyons?" He only partly recognized me and I recognized him not at all. Then I remembered him, a perfectly pleasant fellow from Wharton—finance major, a year behind me. It had been three years. I had been in contact with only one friend from Penn. I tried to smile though I could not remember this one's name. He took the liberty of reminding me and then I knew we had known each other rather well and that I had liked the man. That was so long ago. Clearly he was well launched in his life and probably his career, for which he had been trained, a world for which I too had been trained for four long years, time now worse than useless. He was in another, brighter world and I had no quarrel with that; it was simply a world that did not matter to me, that I had abandoned for another I had not yet glimpsed.

"What . . . what's happened, Nicki?" he asked quietly, genuinely concerned. "Are you all right?"

"Hi, Jack," I said, tentatively.

"You all right, buddy?"

"It's very good to see you, Jack. You look well."

He studied me for a moment, apologized for not introducing his wife, introduced me as an old and dear friend from Penn, looked carefully at my face, and asked if there was anything he could do for me. I told him that I had gone back to school, he asked if I was getting an MBA or a law degree, and I simply smiled and told him that I had switched my interests. As I talked, I realized that my voice cracked, sounded disembodied from disuse. I had a fleeting desire to sit down with them, ask about others we both knew at Penn, ask about his life, explain myself. But I was not into explaining myself and he suddenly remembered that they had a play to catch.

He smiled, said, "Nicki Lyons," told me that they were "in the book," said to call if there was anything I needed, hoped we would meet again soon, perhaps for lunch—but I walked into the crowds and knew I'd never see the man again.

Dick, my one friend from Penn, had been a roommate and close confidant at the college. We had seen each other at Fort Dix and several times in the Village; he had lived with a woman since his Army days and they had an apartment in New York but were planning a drive to the West Coast in a few weeks to live there. We had dinner at a small Italian restaurant on Eighth

Street, I described my little room, and somehow from my sour face and half sentences he read some message in my eyes and abruptly said when we got up: "Stay with us tonight." I wasn't interested in staying with anyone, but he persuaded me and I slept that night in one of their double beds and have been hugely grateful to him since. I was dangerous to myself in those days. Less so after that night when the mere proximity of a friend, the human contact, was healing.

I HAD SAVED several thousand dollars in the Army and I knew that the GI Bill would pay for more schooling, though I did not know how much, so I thought I might wait tables in the Catskills that summer. From an ad, I bought a 1946 black Ford convertible with twin silver exhausts, and drove back to Brooklyn one weekend to pick up more clothing and some books I hadn't been able to carry—some Henry James I knew I'd need for Botsford's last class, Joyce's *Portrait of the Artist as a Young Man*, a Portable edition of Steinbeck I'd bought in the Army, this and that. The visit led to an arrangement for summer work but it was unbearably unpleasant, and I could not get away soon enough and race back to my little room, where I could read again with uninterrupted passion. There was so much I hadn't read and I still had only the faintest sense of what I should do next.

After my last class at the New School, I walked downstairs with Botsford. I had no idea what I wanted to ask him but the term was over and I had to say something to the man. I had hoped that after four months, never missing his course, after reading all the books he assigned and concentrating in every

minute of his classes—which I had never once done at Penn—I
would be different. I did not feel different. I did not feel as if I
were in a new skin. And I did not, in truth, feel a bit smarter. But
there was a new irritation in my brain, odd moments from books
I had read, something pecking away at me. I felt excited by the
magic I faintly glimpsed of what words could do; I felt there was
more I understood and could understand in books I wanted to
read, that I had noted after Botsford mentioned them.

Walking a half pace behind the man I fumbled through the
chaotic darkness of my brain for some words that might give me
a response I desperately wanted to make. Was my work ade-
quate? Had I made progress? Did I have a chance to make the
team? Did I have the brain for this trek on which I'd embarked?
Was it worth my life? Was I at all, even minimally, by nature or by
possibility, even marginally smart enough to wander into these
sacred texts, so far from the world of that old insurance professor who barked about a life being valued in dollars. Was this new
itch I felt, so far beyond dollars, something Botsford thought I
might do with any chance of success? I wanted some kind of
answer, some prescription from this man who appeared to have
answers. I wanted a course of action, a time limit. There was no
chance now, if there ever had been, that I would go back to that
other life, but I still had absolutely no faith that I could survive
in this one. What possibly could I do to pay my way?

Botsford said nothing and I said nothing and in a few
moments we were in the lobby. In one corner, a woman waited
for him. She was dour, stoic, impatient, very attractive. He was
late. He was frequently late. She looked at her watch. Perhaps
he spent too much time with his students. I could see that,
uncharacteristically, he wanted to calm her, explain, and that I
was an impediment. I looked at him and smiled slightly. I was

used to not getting answers and was prepared to leave. I forget if I had mumbled anything on our descent to the lobby. I wanted to say, "You have been my fire striker—but where do I go now?"

I started to say something about my future, then turned to walk away, then turned back when I heard him say, "You've worked hard, but of course you know nothing. What you need, as I told you—instead of random reading, these isolated courses—is an education." He said these words sincerely. He gave me the name of a college upstate, of a contact there; until recently Botsford had taught at Bard. Then he turned from me and said something to the woman that I could not hear. Almost as an afterthought, as if the words might be of some possible use or comfort to me, he said: "Remember. You're not dumb, Nicki. You're just illiterate."

Then he straightened his shoulders, shook his head, wagged a finger at me, took the woman's hand, and bounded off, while I scurried back to my little room and lay on my bed for twenty minutes. Then I got up, began to pack, and headed for my car.

His compliment staggered me.

4

NON SERVIAM

When I had gone back to the house in Brooklyn before the end of the term, I'd found eight or ten people there. I had made the fatal mistake of telling Arthur I would come by to pick up some books and clothing. The former head counselor of a summer camp was loud in one group, and the other men and women were friends or clients of my stepfather's. We had moved from Mount Vernon when I was eleven and we must have owned the two-family house in Brooklyn on East Twenty-fourth Street because I remember the rent check arriving from the Kreismans, who lived in the upper section. They were an older European couple and they had an adult son I rarely saw and a very bright daughter, Dolores, several years older than me; when she heard I had started to read seriously, she gave me a number of books I still have, including the first stories of Kafka I read and a volume of his journals.

The head counselor was some sort of high school administrator for most of the year but had gotten himself into the summer-camp business twenty years earlier, and I remembered him well from the years I had worked at Camp Kee Wah as a junior counselor and waiter. I could see him standing near the flagpole and saluting smartly every morning and evening, and taking the attendance reports from the heads of the various age-groups, in front of the entire camp, like the company commander did when I was in basic training. I could see his ingratiating face introducing the dinners, a play, a banquet, the tribal games that pitted the Iroquois against the Mohawks in running, basketball, volleyball, baseball, swimming, and a dozen other competitions. He had been born for this work. He flourished in front of a young crowd at this summer camp on a small lake in the foothills of the Berkshires. He thrilled to the hum of his own voice. He loved his importance. On variety nights, he now and then demonstrated that he could do a respectable tap dance.

He knew that I had just returned from my Army service and he asked my plans—was I going to enter my stepfather's insurance brokerage? I told him that I was studying other matters, and thought of the chill I'd gotten when Botsford read that passage from Browne's *Religio Medici*, "Life is a pure flame." Why was I back in this house? I was trying to write stories, too, I told him—no, I had had nothing published—and was planning to get a job in the Catskills for the summer, as a waiter, to make bags of money to help me go back to school full-time, as a freshman.

This seemed a radical shift to me, very personal, and I was not prepared to talk further about it. He asked what hotel I was going to work at.

I didn't know yet. I planned to drive up to Monticello or Liberty or Ellenville and stop at several places, just walk in. He shook his head emphatically and said that this could not possibly work. He'd call, then and there, and make arrangements for me. I protested. I'd find my own job. Several men, including my stepfather, came over and the head counselor told them all that I was being very foolish, thinking of driving all the way up to the Catskills to, just like that, get a summer job in the dining room of an important hotel, the kind of high-paying job half the seniors in college wanted. It couldn't be done. My stepfather had called me "foolish" on the last day I visited his house, for wanting to begin college again. I already had a terrific degree from the most prestigious business college in the country and this would be backpedaling. Since I wasn't at all sure that I wasn't being foolish, though I could see no other route to take, I reacted poorly to his analysis. I hoped the head counselor would not use a similar word. I felt I might smash a lamp or a window or kick one of these men. I thought that five months in my little room, pacing, reading, wrapped in books and papers, had insulated me from this world.

"Watch this," the head counselor said.

I stepped back, in the direction of the front door, and felt my stepfather's hand on my shoulder. "Don't be a fool," he said, too loudly. "Let him help. Izzy knows people. And he owes me."

My cheeks were bright red now and I stiffened and promised myself that I would never again come into this house and might not show for the job, if the man got me one.

"It's me, Mo. Sure, Izzy," he said into the phone, motioning to the group of men that now surrounded him, nodding: he'd show them how this sort of thing was done, what sort of influence he had. "How's Lucy?" Pause. "And the boys?"

Did he have a surprise for Mo! A terrific young man. A real mensch. "Full?" he said with incredulity. He couldn't possibly believe that. He knew all about the kitchen at the Nevele. There was always room for one more good young man. "Mo . . . MO, I want . . . Mo, please. Listen to me, Mo. Mo. Mo"—the phone away from his ear now—"this one time. Remember—" And he recounted some old favor he had once done Mo, and then a funny memory they shared. "No, this is absolutely a quality-type person, no schmo. A boy with a degree already . . ."

"From Wharton," my stepfather whispered.

"From the Warner College of Financial Commerce. Have you heard of it, Mo? Then you know."

"Mention the Army," my stepfather said.

"He was in the United States Army . . ."

"Mention the basketball."

"And he played basketball for the Wharton School. Sure. He was a great player, a star. Almost All-American. He could play in the tournament. The guests would love him."

I started to correct the head counselor but my stepfather shook his head from side to side vigorously—I should keep my fucking mouth shut.

"Mo. Mo, listen to me. Would I send you a lemon, a schmuck? There's not a thing whatsoever wrong with him. He could go to a dozen other hotels—the Concord, Grossinger's. Well, I want him to work at the Nevele. I want him to work with you. I told him he'll make more money if he works for you. I want to do *you* this favor, Mo."

I WAS OLDER than all the others in the Nevele barracks, older by several years even then Simon, the law school student I was to work with, a young man quite happy with whom he was. I drove up in my ancient Ford which I had packed with all I owned, all I thought I would ever want to carry with me.

I wanted not to be in a Catskill country-club barracks but I got a corner of the big room and set out my few possessions as neatly as I could in my metal locker—a few clothes, a small box of notebooks and random papers, my library of a dozen or so books. I had brought *Dubliners*, which I had read, and *A Portrait of the Artist as a Young Man*, which I had just started. The stories had shocked me with their care and coiled tensions, and I had glimmers of some haunting match between sound and meaning, the loud noises of "Counterparts" ending with the father beating the son, and the way there was so little dialogue in "The Boarding House," how much the mild lodger was conned with the devastating cunning of an unspoken conspiracy between girl and mother. But I was always hardest on myself in those days and related everything to myself, and it was Gabriel's sight of himself in the mirror, near the end of "The Dead," that struck me hardest, the moment—and I had had a dozen of them, glimpses of my worst fears—when he saw himself for what he was, a ludicrous figure, a well-meaning sentimentalist, a pitiable fatuous fellow.

I began *A Portrait* the night I arrived, amid the raucous chatter, the lewd jokes in the barracks, and could make no sense at all of the baby talk. After the taut intensity of the stories, what sense did this make? That afternoon, Mo—a tall, harried, frowning man—half-sneered at me and said that I would be a busboy and should do everything that Simon, the law student, told me to do. Simon was "a real mensch." He had worked at the Nevele for three summers. He knew exactly what to do, how to act toward the guests. He was liked by everyone. His parents had taken their vacations at the resort from the time he was twelve. He was practically family. He had gotten laid for the first time the summer after his freshman year at Cornell, with an older waitress. He loved the place.

"They're here to be pampered," Simon instructed me. "They've worked hard for their money and they want it to buy them a lot of attention—or their parents did, like mine, and they want you to smile and tell them a joke or two, and to kid them and ask how their day has been, if they shot ninety-five in golf. Small talk is worth the big money around here."

I knew a bit about small clever ingratiating talk. I had heard a lot of it in my home, and at the summer camp, and with the future captains of industry I knew at the Wharton School. At times I had been fairly proficient in the practice. But this reading I'd done, this hunger to change my skin, this longing for something I only vaguely understood, had whacked most of that out of me, and I was trying to be a wise heart rather than a wiseacre, trying to understand not persuade, so everyone around the place thought me standoffish, pretentious. After the first day, Simon took me aside and advised me confidentially, "Kid, you've got to smile more. You're too serious. They don't like it. They think maybe you're looking down on them."

After the second day he said, more forcefully, "Look, you've got something else on your mind and you've got to get it off your mind if you want to survive here. You service the tables all right—glasses, silver, livestock, foul dishes—but no one, not the guests, not even the other waiters and busboys, likes your

attitude. You're dour. They don't want people with a sour attitude around. It's going to cost all of us money, especially me,
so I can't let it continue. Lighten up, will you? I've been trying
to cover for you but . . ."

The thought of this joker covering for me rattled my liver. I
saw him as a man on tracks. He'd take his two-week vacations
here, with his two children. Nevertheless, I tried hard to smile.
It did not at first cost me very dearly to do so and afterward I
had the long afternoons to myself, to read. I tried to play basketball one afternoon but the spirit for the game had quite
gone out of me. I was deep into the *Portrait* now, and was trying strenuously to understand the Catholic drama, that man
on the cross I had seen in my tiny apartment and at the Burt
School. Did anyone, anywhere, really believe in hellfire and
brimstone, and believe that lunatic who outlined the horrors of
an afterlife to teenagers who had dallied with flesh? My own
religion had simply melted. "What have I in common with the
Jews," Kafka asked, as I did, "when I have nothing in common
with myself?" Immortal soul? Obedience to voodoo laws? I was
more worried about whether I could survive another day,
whether I would ever understand a certain paragraph in
Browne's *Urn Burial*, which sent chills through me though I
understood only a few words of it. I sweated profusely when I
read a passage from Joyce and forgot it an instant later. What
other deity could there be but a will to understand, to grow, to
make?

Then, steadily, I began to feel the tug in Stephen to be free
of all fetters, to be gone, away, and I could understand that. So
I skipped back fifty pages and read through them again, more
slowly, and I remembered what I'd read.

For three days I smiled, except when I was alone.

Simon nodded his approval when I asked a singularly noisy guest, in a voice not mine, "There's something I can get for you, Mrs. Jordan?" She wore bright Bermuda shorts, a halter too small for what it restrained, chartreuse lipstick, long earrings, and sungrease to excess.

But by lunch on the fourth day my cheeks hurt too much to smile anymore and two other waiters looked at me and shook their heads as if I were bats or, worse, costing them money. One bad apple could spoil the barrel for all of them. I had finished Joyce that morning, after I'd scraped the breakfast dishes and handed them to Carlos, the dishwasher, my friend; I had read the last dozen pages five times—the confrontation, the declaration, the ringing credo of *non serviam*, of what he would do and what he would not do. The words crowded my brain as I loaded fifteen, eighteen glasses of ice water onto my tray.

"Use a cloth. Don't carry glasses that way," Mo said, but the tray was loaded and I heard him with only a part of my brain and in another moment I was halfway through the swinging doors and I caught: "Don't be a schmuck."

I didn't want to stop in such a dangerous spot, where someone coming in or going out might slam the two-way door into my tray, so I merely tipped up a finger, trying to indicate that he was right, that I'd do it the right way next time. But I was drunk on Joyce and I might well have tipped up my middle finger instead of my pointer. I heard Mo curse—a long, guttural, hopeless kind of curse—behind the closed doors to the kitchen.

As I neared my tables I saw Mrs. Jordan's eighteen-year-old daughter sitting by herself at the family table. Her face behind dark glasses was shiny from the sun and her bare thighs were greasy from sunscreen. Simon had told me only the previous afternoon that she had come on to him the night before and that he was still debating whether or not she was worth the trouble. She was very young. She was sexy but he had no real feeling for her. It might mean a confrontation with Dr. Jordan, or the mother, and a smaller tip. He'd had a dozen such girls over the years—new ones appeared every few weeks, as if on a conveyor belt—and he found no reason to resist them. They were so eager. They were so pretty, so hungry . . .

I looked at the girl's thighs a second longer than I should have looked, Simon's conversation curious to me, and then I felt the glasses on the wet tray begin to wander. I struggled to keep them steady and aimed the tray at the tray stand. Other words began to echo in my head. "I will not serve." The words gathered quickly and pounded against the walls of my skull, and the glasses slipped and slid and I pushed the tray in front of me, the glasses of ice water teetering, made the tray stand, felt the tray slip against my upturned palm, then tripped, fumbled, and saw every last one of the eighteen glasses of ice water careen to the floor, thunderously, splattering their cold contents and shards of glass everywhere. I heard Mrs. Jordan's pretty daughter screech and thought briefly that some of the ice water had surely washed those hot thighs, perhaps even bits of glass. And then, in happy unison, the hundred or so people already in the room, joined by those just entering, shouted, "YEAAA," and began to clap loudly, and then shouted "YEAAA" again, and I made no attempt to pick up anything but simply walked away, out of the dining room and into the kitchen, Joyce out of my head now, and saw Mo slap his head and shake it from side to side slowly, and say, "Schmuck, schmuck, schmuck!" I was not at all sure whether he was referring to himself for having taken me on, or to the head counselor, or to me—the latter, I think.

I marched to the barracks, pushed all my books and clothes into the black 1946 convertible, fled the Nevele, and drove west at demon speed. I filled the radiator with cold spring water in the Utah desert and it got air lock or I would have made it to San Francisco in three days. Whenever I stopped I read from one of the books that was filling me to bursting. I knew with each new paragraph I read that nothing I had written had for a moment created the uncreated conscience of a toad.

5

SCHOOL DAYS

Bard College sat high on a hill overlooking the Hudson River and beyond that the Catskill mountains to the west. The campus was laced with ancient pines, broad fields, stone buildings, and cheap barracks, and the Sawkill Creek cascaded through one side of the property, dropping three or four times in lathed waterfalls, toward the Hudson. The first time I saw the Sawkill I knew it held trout.

Everyone at the college talked incessantly about Rilke and Hölderlin, Jules Supervielle and Trakl, Marx and Yeats and Kafka—though not always the Kafka who had shocked me to the bone but one who had been metamorphosed into concepts and ideas and references I barely recognized. The talk began in

the dining commons at breakfast and there over the black coffee and toast and mess-hall scrambled eggs, it gained force,
perhaps with someone's mention of "Heinrich's seminar," and
gossip about the sighting of the same Saul Bellow whose *Seize
the Day* I had read during a pit stop in Nebraska, and then, like
the peal of a bell, the first "Weltanschauung" of the day, and
several echoes of the word and then quick mention of five stories by D. H. Lawrence that someone named Humphrey had
spoken of, and the talk swept out of the commons and onto the
pebble and macadam paths, howling in my ears, richer, denser
before each class, rising again when the class was over, with
new names, stranger words at lunch, swarming all afternoon
under the maple, an unbroken mantra, the names recurring
like a drumbeat of themes, bleeding finally into the coffee shop
between meals, insinuating itself into Adolph's, a ruddy nearby
bar, for half the night. The talk turned me to stone. I listened
and tried to smile and now and then, stupidly, nodded. I was
petrified that one of these strange young people would start a
conversation with me and pin me to a wall like a butterfly,
throw a sharp word through my heart. At twenty-four I felt as
old as the ancient pines that lined the road to the mansion the
school had recently acquired. Botsford was dead wrong: I was
hopelessly dumb.

Only in the gymnasium, with the familiar basketball in my
hands, the design clear, or whacking the speed bag for all I was
worth, did I feel half alive.

I had interviewed in early June, too late I thought, unless
the school was starved for students. Buzz Gummere, the admis-
sions officer, a tall thin man wearing a neat bow tie and a blue
blazer with gold buttons, was a genuinely pleasant fellow, and
he asked me all manner of questions about what I'd read of

Melville, Hawthorne, Edith Wharton. Nothing. Thackeray? No. What about Yeats. Not yet. But I knew of him and if he gave me two weeks, a month . . . Any of the French novelists? Yes, I'd read a couple of short things by Dostoyevsky. "Russian," he said quietly. We walked here and there on the campus, through the old stone buildings, across the quad, and he mentioned casually that Botsford, who had recommended me highly, would not be coming back after all—"There were some problems"—and why did I want to start again, as a freshman, since I already had an undergraduate degree from a good school like Penn. I told him that I knew nothing. Couldn't he tell? For a moment I could not remember one of those people I had read in Botsford's class, except Jane Austen. "Jane Austen," I said abruptly, in the middle of one of his unrelated questions. "Which novels?" he asked. I said I had read all of them but I couldn't remember the exact titles. "Dickens?" he asked. Nope.

Then he turned to me and said in a genuinely kind voice tinged only slightly with exasperation, "Well, Nick, exactly what have you read?"

"A whole lot of Hemingway. *The Razor's Edge. Martin Eden. Auntie Mame.* Some stories by Salinger. The books Botsford assigned. All of Kafka—the novels, the stories, his letter to his father, two books of his parables, his diaries. Some Henry James, a little. A little Joyce. I like Joyce. I've been reading a lot."

Then Gummere said, with a smile, "Well, that's what I wanted to hear. I'm sure we will have a place for you in the fall. Didn't you say, by the way, that you had . . . full access . . . to your GI benefits?"

On the registration line several months after I had driven to and from San Francisco, worked in an office and picking peaches, I stood behind a tall girl in a sheepherder's coat, with blond frizzy hair; she was part of a little group that was singing "Te pastoi" and other Russian revolutionary songs. She was intensely shy—an art student someone said. The student next door to me in the barracks ran his words together so quickly, so knowingly, that I thought Iliad-Odyssey-Aeneid was the name of one book. I knew better a week later and also that Gerta, Go-etha, and Goth were only one writer whose name I'd never heard. I pushed my reading that way: by jotting down any unfamiliar name I heard, I had, by October, a slew of names and words on lists and index cards and napkins and matchbook covers on my walls—books to be read, authors to research, words to be defined or learned, often by repeating them, finding sentences in which to write them a dozen times. I began to write again—critical essays, some poems, a few very autobiographical stories, vaguely disguised, and now and then I caught a very faint glimmer in all the high pretentious rhetoric of a voice that hinted, vaguely, a glimmer was all, of being my own—though whenever I felt I was somewhat near a place where I should be, something would kick me in the kidneys. Once, in November, professor and poet Ted Weiss gave me a manuscript of his new poems to deliver to Heinrich Blücher in my old Ford, and I read the first page of his poems ten times, whenever I stopped, sweating, bewildered that after nearly three months in this place I still could not look a fresh poem in the face and tell the slightest thing about what it meant. In this case I was reading the contents page, without page numbers. And of what I wrote myself, it more and more sounded forced, jingling.

I read stories with Bill Humphrey, often walking along the

banks of the Sawkill. He was remarkable in his ability to retell a story almost word for word, understand how a phrase anticipated its echo, its later resolutions, how a dozen such phrases caught you up in a symphonic net that would not release you until its hold was resolved. He knew exactly when a theme was revealed, when that theme modulated into another key. He never used notes, rarely carried a book, and the stories were soon etched on my brain—stories by Faulkner, Joyce, Lawrence, Hemingway, Flannery O'Connor, Henry James, and half a dozen others. Once, when we were talking about "The Real Thing," I looked down at the creek and to get back some of my own said that I thought I could write about rivers and trout better than James. Humphrey shook his head and said, "No, you couldn't," and then quoted that line about James being a writer on whom nothing was lost, and added, "not even rivers."

The voluble Ted Weiss brought an embracing enthusiasm to a class called The Common Course, which covered the Bible through later major works. He spent a full two weeks on the phrase "in the beginning was the word," and in each class ranged fluidly from the Bible to the Greeks to his beloved Shakespeare, about whom he wrote *The Breath of Clowns and Kings*. His own breath filled my lungs and when, several years later, I began to teach, I kept hearing echoes of his voice and spirit course through me. I loved the man and disagreed with him only when he said once that I tried too hard, that I put too much of a burden on myself; I still thought I didn't try half hard enough and that only my greatest efforts would bring fruit.

At Bard I took a recalcitrant wheel and with maximum torque set it briskly in motion. I found a small tough flame, at last, in the corner of my damp straw, and fanned it to a fury, and that fire became a force and also a cleansing. I found, in the inscrutable texture of myself, places I had not realized existed, places worth seeding, windows that would open. My memory changed. So much began to stick like glue. Is the rhetoric too high? Are the metaphors mixed? The miracle of the thing astounded me. I read everything, day and night. I learned to sit for ten hours, studying and writing, and I could feel my mind becoming more agile, aware, connected, as I had found my body in training grow the skills I had needed to play basketball. I found Whitman and Emily Dickinson and the poetry of Donne and Marvel and Hopkins and Shakespeare and Chaucer and even the Bible, which I had fled. Jane Austen's violins now played in sharp antiphony to Kafka, and they were just as important to me. Kafka, who had been all, became only part of the tapestry, though always more than a narrow specialist in impossibilities. Faulkner led me to Twain, Twain back to Hemingway; then only a few Hemingway stories survived, the early ones. Back and forth I traveled the strings of this new loom, weaving some odd fabric of my spontaneous design, for my own uses, which I still did not quite understand.

But now it stuck. The pieces of some crazy puzzle began to fit into recognizable sections. I began to glimpse a whole. I found ancestors who were not blood; I began to take possession of an inheritance I thought I had squandered. I found a memory that held. I changed my permanent address to that of the college.

It was not so much a good or even a productive year as an essential year—one that changed me more than any other, one that began to chart a course. From terror and abject doubt, from fears that numbed memory, my mind shifted in fits and quickenings to that which was self-feeding, self-protecting, self-sustaining. Not every book told me its secrets or told me what I wanted to know but more and more did, in some incrementing fashion: having understood Milton, somehow I understood Dickens more; having worked my way into the metaphysical conceits of Donne—watching the palpable compass open and lean after the other foot, which traveled—I began to enter the worlds of Hopkins and Eliot and Stevens; having suffered among the pure uncrudded breasts of Spenser, I found the treasures of a dozen other poets mysteriously unlocked.

Bard was a place of rabid talk, compulsive reading, the bright silver of the river through old bent pines at sunrise when I went to fish it alone—my one escape from the terror of all that talk—the long gray hills and somber woods in winter, the old stone buildings, new worlds exploding in my head every day, a radical intensity that burned off the dullness of ivy, worn-lichen-covered rocks near a waterfall, and the first pink-white buds on the Hudson Valley apple trees. I found trout in the Sawkill and love finally for that tall girl with frizzy hair—mysterious, stubborn, independent, utterly devoted to her painting, shy, passionate, encouraging, gentle, wise.

Often in the long evenings of late spring we drove on the River Road, which ran for six or seven miles from the college to the Rhinecliff train station, past a dozen old estates fronting the Hudson. Tentatively at first we began to explore each other's world and dreams, inching closer, dreams soon bleeding into each other's, taking on the faint shape and form of odd disjointed plans and hopes. We both wanted a large loose careless family, something far from our own early days. Perhaps five or six children. Perhaps on Ibiza, perhaps in Maine. A lot of children and a total devotion to painting and writing, open to all the arts. Maybe the children would play instruments. We wanted music. Mari had already shown her work in a Woodstock gallery and the artist Philip Guston, whom she admired, had left an appreciative note. I had written precisely nothing but a few very personal, very half-baked stories and some clumsy attempts at poetry. We both wanted things, objects—small or large, mostly cheap, most not shop-bought, chosen with care, with some call on our affections, our friends as the cold sets of furniture and decorations of our parents' homes were never friends. Now and again we would riff on some imagined part of this life. A small studio grew to be one large enough to welcome twelve-foot canvases, dozens of them. Four—no, eight—skylights. Six—no, ten—easels. Dozens of huge well-stretched canvases, made with the best linen. Stacks of paint tubes with names like cadmium red, cobalt violet, Mars brown, emerald green. Cans of paint. Wasn't there a paint maker's shop in Paris, near the Grande Chaumière—Foinet, Lucien Lefebvre-Foinet, that was it. We'd only buy paint there. Then one of us would lean over and softly touch the other's hand. We'd smile. We'd grow quiet and look over and smile again. I'd write from my heart, perhaps important books. The children would all recite Yeats by age six. Sometimes we'd drive the length of the River Road, then back to school, then drive back and forth again, and again.

And then one evening in late May when shadows had darkened the surrounding old pines and hemlock, and we sat in a little pocket of light from the nascent moon, like Levin I confessed my multitude of sins and fallings-off, my numbing doubts and fears, a litany of every reason I could find to disqualify myself from any permanent liaison. I told her all, and I was terrified.

She was silent for several minutes. I did not dare look at her. I had said too much. I could take nothing back, ever, and all was lost.

Then at last she turned to me and touched my cheek and smiled and said, "Well, I guess you're my fate, old mole."

THERE IS A photograph of us, taken more than sixty years ago at our wedding in California. We had married that year on September first at her parents' house in Menlo Park. We look very young and obscenely happy. My mother was there, wearing a rose corsage, and my half-sister, Amie, then fifteen; my stepfather, Arthur, appears faintly in that photograph, a ghostly reflection in a glass window. Mari's father, a very tall cattle rancher, had wanted to "have some of the boys dig a pit in the backyard and roast half a cow," but her mother, transplanted from Riverside Drive during the Depression, wouldn't have it. My old friend Dick, now living in Berkeley, was my best man.

Mari had been accepted for the master's program in painting at Cranbrook Academy, in Bloomfield Hills, Michigan, and after we were married and had gone to New York City to collect my few worldly goods, we headed west. I had thought of returning to Bard but it had done all I could allow it to do. Although I had fared better there academically than I had ever done in college classes, my highest grade was only a B, and I had only narrowly passed a music appreciation course. I loved Mozart and Bach, Haydn and the lyrics of Purcell—but could not muster an intelligent word about any of them. In Michigan we found an apartment in an old Victorian mansion on Woodward Avenue, not far from Cranbrook, with a half dozen other graduate students, some married, a few still among our closest friends. We rented what had been the kitchen and sun porch and maid's room.

I checked a map and saw that there were several colleges in Detroit, an hour away, and that the University of Michigan was about the same distance, down the Pontiac Trail. The university sounded like the better place so, after we settled in, I called the English Department there and made an appointment to see if I couldn't parlay my degree in insurance, my five months at the New School, and my year as a freshman at Bard into acceptance into the master's program.

Harry Ogden was the first academic dragon I met. He was the author of a narrow scholarly book on the garden in seventeenth-century literature—or some such. He stood at the entrance to the great cave, with all of its riches—a tall, thin man with great gray bushy eyebrows and a sculpted sneer—and either let you in or melted you with his fiery breath. I was a new breed in the late fifties, though I saw myself as a part of no breed. To him I was simply an encroaching Hebrew, untutored in Latin or Greek, lousy even at French, without a tie, wearing sneakers, long overdue for a haircut well before everyone under thirty needed one, with burning eyes and a fierce zeal to be let into the feast. I had nibbled at the great feast. I'd liked the taste. About that—if not about anything else—I had no ambiguity.

"Go back, Mr. Na-than Lyons," Ogden said in a slow bass whisper, when I had explained my case, my past, my hopes. "Go back. Way back"—he waved his hands easterly, in the general direction from which I had come—"before it is too late. You are not adequately prepared. I can say with assurance that you will not graduate from this place."

I told him, sententiously, that I was much less interested in graduating than in learning.

"Ah, yes. Learning. But the point is that you cannot succeed here, Mr. Na-than Lyons," he said in a warm fatherly way. "Go back"—and his voice dropped a register for this confidential bit of advice—"to the garment district."

A year earlier and I would have been burned to a crisp. But he was too late. I merely asked him with a smile what steps I needed to take to be admitted into the program. He sighed, looked slowly from my wild hair to my old sneakers, and sent me for a seven-hour battery of tests, Rorschach to aptitude. The former spooked me. Someone would be taking a microscope to my brain, fishing around in all of my dark eddies.

Two days later, when he examined the results, he frowned, shook his head, and said reluctantly that I could take four courses as a "special student" and if I earned four A's there was a chance, some slight chance, that he would be "compelled" to let me into the sacred temple.

That long winter—nearly freezing every night like the coffee we once left in a cup that froze solid; rocketing down the Pontiac Trail every morning as if it were a bobsled course, after the milkman got my motor started; straining my brain at night to learn Middle English and linguistics—I got them: four, my first college A's. Only one course was an unalloyed delight: Nineteenth-Century Russian Literature, taught by a young man named John Mersereau. He was wise, ordered, patient, witty, and his love of the great Russians was infectious. For the first time in a classroom I sat on the edge of my chair, my hand almost constantly upright, as anxious to talk publicly about Raskolnikov and Levin and Alyosha as I had been to read three or four times the number of books assigned. I could not get enough of the energy, the intensity of the Russians, and Mersereau often smiled, as if he had been there before with these books, and nodded for me to speak when I could barely hold in the words. I had been silent in all classes before this but now found my tongue and was always curious to talk about everything I was reading. His A had a plus beside it, the only one, he said, he'd ever given. Years later, many years later, I wrote to thank him. They had been intensely busy years. He had died five months earlier.

When I returned, Ogden sighed wearily. Not Na-than Lyons again! He looked over my papers, smiled faintly, shook his head, and said that he could find no reason to keep me from registering for the master's program but that he frankly held out no hopes for me. He had no official reason to bar me, he said, but personally, he thought I might find something more suitable in New York City. Might I be persuaded to do that, he asked.

I summoned one last smile, from my smiling childhood, shook my head, and quietly said, "No."

We moved from Pontiac to Ann Arbor later that spring, after Mari had finished her master's and I had spent my first months in the graduate program. We rented a small white clapboard house and Mari delivered our first child, Paul, in July.

I found one great teacher that fall, Austin Warren, and he became my mentor, a man who lived inside me for years. I took a course on the baroque poets with him, another on translation, one on his New England saints, and eventually he directed my dissertation on the most minor of minor New England saints, Jones Very. His classes were memorable and haunting seminars around one long table. He was a short man, always impeccably dressed, with a deep voice and a unique twitch in his neck, which he seemed to use for emphasis as he circled the table slowly behind us; he gave an especially prolonged and visceral twitch when he spoke of the sweet wounds in a Crashaw poem. Emily was Saint Emily; Donne was superior to that generalist Shakespeare; he anointed not only New England saints but his own church of local saints and martyrs. Often, he laughed a deep and guttural laugh at his own wit. Now and again he would call me at four or five in the morning and say something like, "I have been reading Father Caussade, Nathan, and I thought you should hear this passage," and he would read for ten minutes, sighing and chuckling now and again, and then abruptly ask, "Did I call you or did you call me? God bless you, Nathan," and the phone would click. He was the most compelling of teachers, the most exacting, and I was drawn into his world, wrapped in it, and I remained his devoted student for half a dozen years after I left Ann Arbor, even finding his words and mannerisms vying with my own voice and the voices of Ted Weiss and Bill Humphrey in my own classroom, in another state, another world, until all of them faded.

The program at Michigan was measured, cohesive, and it added order to my chaotic brain. G. B. Harrison's two-semester Shakespeare, though I could hardly control myself merely listening to him read those long-fixed lectures to a class of hundreds, hearing his papal pronouncements like *"Antony and Cleopatra* is Shakespeare's most beautiful play," yet offered that balance, gave me the frame, the overview in which to hold the barrage of books I was reading. Another lecture course by a famous medievalist regularly put a large class to sleep as with head lowered he read from his set of yellowed notes—until once he actually laid his old head down on the podium. We all awoke. Had he died, in the middle of his own lecture? The room went dead silent. But after a few moments he rose, looked out over the group, and with little modulation in his voice, reread a paragraph he had read before he went for his rest. Once, with a wry smile, he said in the middle of his reading, "And then there's the Miller's Tale"—but he never discussed it. I studied the romantic novelists with Sheridan Baker and some twenty-five years later, when one of my sons took a class with him, Baker remembered the essay I had written on *Emma*.

I began to feel so fucking cocky that, in the MA program, I did this on a multiple-choice test on the Civil War: the third or fourth question, out of some hundreds, offered five options for the answer to "What was the single most important cause of the war?" and each of them was a good strong cause, so I wrote a ten-page essay on why the question was misguided, even absurd, why they were all interlocking "causes," and did not answer any other questions; I gratefully accepted a C for the course. Ah, grades. They had meant nothing to me for so very many years and in many ways still did not, but I welcomed some kind of acknowledgment, some measurement now, for all I was doing and settled for those bland letters, from that C to all A's to one A-plus.

But, oh, I had gone too quickly—how casually, blithely I had skipped along, hewing to what moved me, with vast gaps and untutored passions. Too fast. Too fast.

I FINISHED MY master's and doctorate in less than four years. In a short time we had an infant, Charlie, and a toddler, and somehow I began to scorch my past. I had a new life growing. In an old drum in our backyard I burned the journal I made in the Army, thinking it would profit no one to see the ugly thing now—and only recently wished I still had it. To earn money, I took in typing and then was given two freshman English classes to teach. The great surprise, when I stepped into a classroom from the other side of the room for the first time—after years of despising school, then turning mad for learning—was not only that I could talk to a group of young people about what I had grown to love but that I loved to do so. In front of a class, my mind—crammed with all the plots and people and words— took flight. I was drunk on the words. I had been able to remember nothing five years earlier, not even the titles of books I had just read, and now all of it was available to me, whole paragraphs of prose from a story, long sections of poetry. The miracle of it: a brain alive, a brain that remembered!

That first day I talked and talked more, saying just about everything I knew—about basketball and my Army years and Kafka and Shakespeare and Melville and the recent births of my children, and it all was larded with Emerson's maxims and pickled in odd anecdotes from my Brooklyn childhood.

Some students tried to take notes and gave up. Some smiled and even chuckled to one another. I felt their presence, tugging more and more out of me, and I tried to keep some order to it, though that was quite impossible with my brain rampaging like a creek in spring flood. Finally I stopped for a moment, looked around the classroom, and asked if there were any questions.

There were none. So I took a fleeting glance at my watch and saw that a full eighteen minutes had elapsed during my diatribe. "Well, we'll leave early today," I said, after I had given them handouts. "See you all on Thursday."

They smiled and laughed and gathered their books and in a few moments the room was empty.

When I looked down for a moment, I saw that my fly was wide open.

THE LAST YEAR went quickly and toward the end of the second semester Mari was pregnant again, with our third child in three years. We lived in that little white house in Ann Arbor, Mari exhibited her paintings at the Forsythe Gallery and sold out her first show, I read and typed and taught, and the year vanished. Sometime that spring I began to teach with far less chaos and with focused passion, and by April I began to apply for a number of teaching positions. Austin Warren was eager for me to go to Ohio, where one of his other students taught, or upstate New York, where I'd been offered a position in one of the state colleges; he thought New York City a Gomorrah.

In the end, I took a job at Hunter College for $100 a week as an adjunct, drove straight to New York that June with an old Rambler stuffed with books, paintings, and the few possessions we had not shipped or given to friends, two colicky babies and a wife seven months pregnant, and plunged like fate into that great cold tumultuous city of Mannahatta.

6

SOME WOODSTOCK SUMMERS

Several summers during the mid-sixties we rented a bare-bones cottage in Woodstock called "The Studios," one of the original buildings left in the old Byrdcliffe colony, built not long after the turn of the nineteenth century—Mari and I and our four hyperactive children, four years spanned the first to last, the oldest seven our first summer. We had been in New York for several years and teaching was my only job, though what I earned was not nearly enough to support a family of six in New York City. I owed increasing sums of money to banks and schools and a few friends and Dan's cigar store on the corner of Broadway and Eighty-fifth Street. I knew I'd have to find a second job soon, perhaps a third, and in time I did. Woodstock was before all that.

Peter Whitehead, son of Byrdcliffe's founder, charged us $300 from the time the crocuses came to when it got too cold for the potbellied stove to warm our toes, though we used it only during the summer months. At night raccoons scratched at the garbage cans and our sleep was rattled by the snap and plunk of mouse traps set along the two-by-four-inch raw rafters eight feet up; the traps bounced down when tripped. The place was lousy with mice. I baited the traps with peanut butter and killed dozens of them that first summer, with impunity.

Mari painted, I wrote critical essays, which I placed with half a dozen literary magazines, the children ran amok, like the mice. Marlon Brando passed us on his motorcycle on the thruway; I fed the raccoon and it mistook my finger for a hot dog; we watched Dylan and Baez ride back and forth on Tinker Street on their motorcycles, buoyantly young, the world poised to embrace them. Dell Raley, Tina Bromberg, and some of the Malkine children—it often took two to handle our four— helped with our kids. We kept warm with slab wood we bought from a young farmer who gave us four ducklings; with the colossal stupidity of a city boy, I thought young ducks would surely like to swim and put them in a bathtub—for what was their final swim. I leaned toward moving water whenever we drove past the Sawkill or Esopus and bolted from Byrdcliffe to fish whenever I could. The essays I had published were about Kafka, Thomas Nashe, Chrétien de Troyes, Saint Augustine, Tolstoy, Melville—but they bore the faint stink of graduate school work; my dissertation on Jones Very had been published by Rutgers University Press, and I had seen a dozen of my poems find homes in literary quarterlies. Somehow none of it counted. I was restless. I still got every story and poem rejected from major magazines across the country and kept filling the shoeboxes I had kept from my lonely days in that tiny room.

One day in mid-August I set out alone for the old Laurel House in Haines Falls, where I had spent summers from the time I was born through those gray years at the Burt School. Mari was working well and preferred a house free of the *click-clack* of my Underwood Standard, and the children were all at a local day camp. I drove through nearby Palenville, then up twisting Route 23A, past the spot where you could glimpse the famous Kaaterskill Falls, the little town of Haines Falls, and then east toward the dirt road that led to the hotel. At first I could not find the road. I recognized nothing. My head was a hive of worries—money worries, worries about what I was writing. I may have missed the turn. I had taken wrong turns before. Had the course of the road shifted? I remembered a view off to the left when my cousins and I marched to Tannersville, singing, "Row, row your boat," but trees obscured the view now.

"Laurel House Road."

Even at fifteen miles an hour I almost missed the foot-long faded sign, and the dirt path that looked exactly like so many of the others I had passed. I braked hard, backed up a few dozen feet, and made a sharp turn down the suddenly familiar road and felt the wheels skid on the dirt and the car swivel. The nine-hole golf course would come first, where we all picked blackberries and raspberries in August, and then at the crest of the hill, where the clubhouse was, I might be able to see the high white columns of the hotel and the circular drive in front of it with its ring of lilac bushes that were always spotted with purple when we came up each June. I paused for a moment. In my mind I could see the shack in which my white-bearded grandfather butchered the chickens that arrived almost daily on a big truck filled with dozens of wooden cages, each crammed with squawking white birds fated for the hotel dining tables; and in the shack: feathers fly furiously—blood on him, on me, on the sawdust floor where birds still flopped. I could see my uncles with their great hairy chests playing pinochle in the sun on the back porch; the tire swing and the compost pile behind the kitchen, where I dug worms; the swimming pool and behind it the creek, always silver-green, icy cold, and clear as water from a tap. And where the creek headed downstream to the great Kaaterskill Falls that marked the end of Grandpa's property, there was an observation deck and nearby a very wide flat rock with hundreds of names carved into it, dating from the mid-nineteenth century. I had put my name there, too—Nicki Ress.

Memories mingled with emotions, so much a part of the fabric of my bone and blood that I found myself prying them loose, one by one. There had been a midnight supper one year, an anniversary or birthday of some sort—I couldn't remember whose—and I could see those glorious swans of ice being carved that afternoon and the platters of cold cuts and bowls of fruit, and then my grandfather with happy glossy eyes, a patriarch, there on the dais, surrounded by hundreds of family and friends. The main course might have been steak but my family always ate chicken—chicken lunch and dinner, every day—and the next morning I slept until eleven-thirty after the midnight supper, and my cousins and I talked about it for weeks.

Mostly I remembered the lake and the creek, where I spent every hour I could, where I could catch anything that moved—back-darting crayfish, newts, grasshoppers, perch, pickerel, and little frogs. I remembered it all starkly but piecemeal and could not put the parts or the years into their proper places—when what happened, where it all stood in relation to everything else. I remember the hotel comedian Pitzy Katz giving me nickels for frogs he now and then put under the overturned coffee cups at every table.

But there was no golf course around the bend. When I made the turn and came to another halt I saw only a lightly wooded field. I parked along the roadside and walked through grass fields over two feet high, I could see no mounds that might have been the greens, and the entire area was sprinkled with new trees, most of them small, no more than three or four feet high, mostly poplars and birch, rising above the grass and brambles. It was impossible to conceive where the golf course might even have been.

In the small clubhouse after the season, a couple of us kids often found golf balls, tees, a broken club or two, as much as a few dollars in loose change. In that lower corner of the field, near the road, I could see that there was now no structure whatsoever—so I walked to where the building had been, got out, and bent over. Nothing. No sign that any structure had been there—only the pervasive shrubs, sproutlings, high grasses. And no sign of the huge red barn that had stood to my left. Logs blocked the road here, and from the logs and the neglect of the golf course, and the condition of the road, I knew that the hotel—already a hundred-year-old relic when my grandfather owned it—would be unused, neglected, fallen into disrepair. But it would be good to see those large white columns, the great circular drive, the old porch in the back, that world that had been my childhood every long summer from before memory until I was eight.

I took a few steps to the right, looked, and it was not there.

I looked again, down into the hollow where the hotel had been for a hundred years, and saw only a tangle of high grasses and brush, small poplars, birches, and pines. There were half a dozen mountain laurel bushes. There was no hotel.

I walked quickly now, down into the hollow that, on a Fourth of July or Labor Day, had once teemed with people I knew, many of them family: uncles, aunts, cousins, friends of my uncles and aunts whom I also called "uncle" or "aunt," my old grandparents from Pinsk. There would be Dodges and Buicks parked in the road that led to the falls; children playing in the sandbox behind the back porch; that interminable pinochle game; dozens of people in the circular driveway, talking, laughing, heading up the hill to play golf or to the old concrete swimming pool; people arriving and hugging old friends, English interspersed with Yiddish everywhere, people chatting with animation, laughing at some old story. I knew them all. The same ones came back every year and I was related, somehow, to every one of them, all family.

I ran the last forty yards down the hill and was soon walking on the exact ground on which the great white hotel had stood. Nothing. A few boulders. Several clumps of fading tiger lilies. Saplings. Clumps of high weeds. Brambles, tangled and untended. I thought I remembered where a neat grove of lilac bushes once stood, off to the right, in a cluster of thirty or forty trees. I saw three, past their bloom. I walked slowly over the humps in the ground, pushing away the high timothy and weeds with my feet, looking down at the roots of all this dense growth for some specific sign, any sign, that this was exactly where the hotel had been. I found none. The land was wild.

There was not one indication, anywhere, that the Laurel House or any other human structure had existed in this place.

Only the falls were where I knew they would be—the flow less than I remembered but the same crystalline creek, flowing out of the heavy pine and hemlock forest, down over the slate-bottomed pools, over the great cleft and plunging down into the awesome clove. The space stretched out, and then farther out and down, and I felt that hollow twinge in my loins that I had always felt when I was a boy and played too close to the brink of this ledge, and I looked out across the illimitable space, across the clove, toward the intersecting mountains in the far distance, cobalt, mauve, and Payne's gray, layered, textured, growing dimmer as they receded farther into the distance until I could see them no more. I searched the rocks for my name but could not find it among the hundreds of others; perhaps the water, in spring torrents, had washed it away. I had been seven years old when I scratched it into the stone and perhaps had not dug deeply enough.

The entire hollow had returned to some primitive state. The forest had claimed back most of its own. It was as if nothing of my past existed at all. With difficulty I found the rudiments of a path I knew led to the lake, which skirted the thin creek that took water from a few scant feeders and from the overflow of the lake. Before long I turned to the left and came to a place I knew well. The creek was merely a trickle and there were only a few boards downstream and in the brush that might suggest a bridge had been here. Three support posts remained. I looked at the nearly barren little spot, without enough water to hold even a few minnows, for a long time. Then I turned to head back to the car and the return trip to

Woodstock. On the way I began to remember every small detail of a day so many years earlier, slowly, in the sequence it had taken place, until I captured—and now wanted to capture again—the great trout.

There was a story in that first trout and I had started to write about it but the voice was still academic, flat, and the incident itself had been much earthier, with a life of its own, if I could regain it.

The summer had already yielded a piece of piscatorial prose. A friend had introduced me to Jimmy Mulligan, who drew cartoons for the *New Yorker*, and Jim began to talk of a mythic friend, Frank Mele, a violist and remarkable fly fisher. A proposed fishing trip with him kept being postponed on slim grounds and that managed to triple the mystery of the man. Then, a week before I drove to the Laurel House, I finally set off with Frank and Jim to the Beaverkill River—"Mecca" for fly fishers, Frank said. He was a gaunt man with dark, old blinking eyes, stunning pronouncements, Delphic and hilarious, and with all the pit stops and Delphic pronouncements, the hour-and-a half trip was accomplished in nine hours. By then I could barely stand, let alone pitch a fly. Frank promptly caught two large trout, Jim and I nothing. The day was so pungent, unique, unforgettable that I promptly sat at my old typewriter and it wrote itself at one sitting.

Somewhere in the writing of that shaggy-fish tale about that long circus of a trip I felt a new voice that sounded far from the academic cant I had learned too well in graduate school and also from the pretentious, stilted prose I had written and thought was literature. I sent it right into the world, and then, when I returned from Haines Falls, I finished my little story about the big trout I had gigged in the creek that tumbled over Kaaterskill Falls, writing a story that had crouched in my brain for decades in a four-hour rush.

In these stories, especially the second, writing about something I had loved for so long, I found a voice that was earthy, nimble, wry, full of wit and worms and celebration, free from pretension and preaching or analyzing, all that was fancy-dan or trendy. That second story had in it the mud of the creek and the point of the long-shank hook with which I gigged that trout. I had lain on the weathered boards of an old bridge, watched a dimpling sunfish, seen the nose of a great spotted fish protruding from under the base of the bridge, tried for it without success, and then eased the hook, strapped to an alder branch, into its mouth, and yanked. It was more vivid after my trip up the mountain and back to the hotel, and altogether different from anything I had read or written before.

In a week I got back a one-sentence note from the editor of *Field & Stream* advising me in his own hand (I'd thought these editors had forgotten how to use them): "We like 'Mecca' and a check for $1,000 will go out to you next week." I nearly peed in my pants. A few weeks later, just after we had returned to the city, the other was accepted, too. I sent them to my friend Emile Capouya, then publisher of Funk & Wagnalls, and he urged me to do a book, in the vein of the two stories, a "mélange of poetry and technology." I wrote *The Seasonable Angler*, he published it, and over the next years I wrote a number more, some with illustrations by Mari on the jacket and in the interior. What fun it all was!

The stories and books were miles from the literature I had found late in my young life and had begun to teach with such passion--but they were my own and were the beginning of something. I wrote Austin Warren about them and proudly

sent him *The Seasonable Angler*, but he advised me sternly that
I must at once abandon all this piffle about trout and attend to
my academic duties, my true career, which he had prepared me
for. Sadly, I wrote him an intemperate letter that I have long
and painfully regretted, telling him that I rather liked trout and
thought mayflies—especially *Ephemera guttulata*—were not piffle, and that I felt immensely comfortable with the romp of
these stories I had found that long last summer in Woodstock
and was proud of this new direction.

And then, the city demanding more and more attention
lest it devour me, I took a second and then a third full-time job
and tried by hook or crook to keep on those tracks I'd laid during my Catskill summers until we could circle back to
Woodstock, much later.

7

THE FIRE AT 20 WEST

Our first apartment, at 20 West Eighty-fourth, was soon filled with books, paintings, objects of all kinds that we had bought at street fairs and church bazaars. It was far from Ibiza and, with all the children, too close already. We had moved there directly from Ann Arbor and loved the Upper West Side and the happy chaos of our digs. I had begun to teach at Hunter College and then had taken a second job in publishing. One cold and windy December afternoon I was at Crown Publishers, where I had recently started as a proofreader with permission from Hunter College to shift into the night session so I could take on a day job. About three, Mari called, abject hysteria in her voice. "The apartment . . . fire . . . everyone all right. Come quickly, Nick. Come quickly."

I caught a cab outside the offices, kept wishing it to go faster, and when I got to Central Park West and Eighty-fourth Street there was a circus of smoke and sirens and lights and fire engines, with firemen rushing in and out of our building. Mari exploded out of the huge crowd, hugged me, and repeated four or five times that the children were safe. Paul, Charlie, and Jenny had been in school; Tony, then three, had been carried down a back staircase from the sixth floor by a savvy babysitter; a collie that had been given to us by a friend in Woodstock had bolted back into the far bedroom and died of smoke inhalation.

It was a flash fire—very fast and very hot. Swept by the wind. An angry drug dealer had torched the old Episcopal church next door and flames had buffaloed out of the brick-and-wood building at the level of our apartment. The minister had been active in trying to rid the neighborhood of drugs.

We settled that night into one large room in a nearby hotel, the six of us, and two days later I went back. We had grown to love the apartment and our dog, Honey. Mari and I slept in the dining room, there were two small bedrooms for the children, and Mari painted in the bigger back bedroom. Most of the work she had done since she was twelve or so was in the apartment. The policeman's light flicked through the dark dank rooms and I saw the paintings first: those on the walls, still hanging by their wire, attached to nails. The stretcher bars were blackened and tilted crazily but intact; the canvases were burned through, ripped open and curled, and what was left, raw and shredded, was black. The oil paint had gone first and the impatient fire had scorched what it could touch quickly and swept on.

Our combined library of art and literature, then about eight hundred books, had been our great joy. The top rows of books were bloated from water and were lost; many of the others were partly waterlogged, and all were touched by fire or smoke. We later picked through them one at a time and saved about fifty; a half century later the few we had kept were gray from the fire and still stank of smoke. Not a piece of furniture was salvageable, the stink of wetness and smoke in all of it.

A metal box that held all of our birth certificates, the children's shot records, our marriage license, some insurance contracts, papers of that stripe, had been cracked open by a fireman's pick. The papers were seared, burned at the edges, but I could save some of them. My father-in-law's Patek Philippe watch had been swiped by one of the firemen.

I smiled when I saw that a chicken in the refrigerator's freezer was cooked well enough to eat; and my Underwood Standard typewriter was a ragged lump of molten metal. The only novel I have ever tried to write was burned to a crisp and deserved its fate. As in my earlier stories, the dozen characters in it, all with some different hair color or height, perhaps a nose wart and crossed eyes, spoke and acted like clones of their author. It was called *Fire in the Straw*.

No Alexandria, I thought—but warm enough for me.

It was a pretty thorough piece of work and the fire never paused to give my new fishing tackle special consideration. I had begun to fish again and had become deliriously passionate about fly-fishing, that most absorbing of piscatorial pursuits. Even thinking about rivers and their speckled denizens was a happy place to be after long days in the city. The closet door in my little study was seared through and inside my vest hung loosely from a wire hanger, nearly burned away. Several plastic boxes had been chewed through, the flies singed, their feathers gone. My waders were a lump of melted rubber; my old wicker creel was a small black skeleton on a rear nail; a favorite well-worn felt hat was a mere bit of rag; and a whole shelf of well-used angling knickknacks had collapsed and lost itself in the wet, black mulch on the floor. Three aluminum rod cases were roasted black and the bamboo rods inside them had all oozed glue, swollen grossly and beyond further use.

Loss of the paintings by my intrepid brilliant wife hurt for years. I had barely been able to look at the ghosts on the walls, eviscerated, askew, curled like half-burned paper. All her passion and skill and training had lived in those paintings. In the end we could save only a few that the fire had merely breathed on; another few we tried to salvage but could not. One was out for framing, and I had two in my office at Crown.

Fire, the great liquidator, had cleansed almost everything we had built and left only memories and a great hollowness. We could not think of what to do but begin again. Mari found a couple of floors in a brownstone and within ten days we moved there with six green contractor bags full of stuff that stank of fire. It was too small but we lived there, first the six of us, then Mari and me, for forty-five years.

8

HUNTER NIGHTS

The man who later became president of the college was in charge of the freshman-composition program at Hunter College in the Bronx when I started to teach full-time, bright-eyed, after finishing my doctorate at Michigan. Leonard was what is commonly called "a nice guy," a man with a relaxed and comfortable style toward both student and teacher, tall, thin, with sandy hair never fully combed, affable, not especially smiling but sincere and interested. I could not imagine that he either enjoyed or read the books that had so recently inflamed my whole being, spreading through me like ink in water. But if he was not passionate about ideas, neither was he ever overtly their enemy. He liked a friendly game of poker, with beer and pretzels and old colleagues. He liked the hum of a nice intellectual conversation now and then; an art book with plenty of color illustrations pleased him; he relished the game of college politics, which I have never understood; curious conscience never troubled his sleep.

He monitored the lower-level adjuncts and instructors warmly. He was kind, fair, and helpful regarding our personal lives, practical in his advice. "You really spend six to eight hours marking a set of student papers?" he asked incredulously. It took me at least that amount of time. I tried to look at each word, each sentence, to watch the development of the thesis, the proofs, the voice. Ridiculous, he thought. He was trying to save me. He spent no more than an hour and a quarter, maximum: a few circled errors concerning spelling or agreement, a mixed metaphor (marked "MM"), a dangling participle ("dp"), and a two-line comment overall—that was enough. Too many comments, he sincerely believed, would only confuse them. Where did I think I was—Harvard?

He was a comfortable man to be with, and since this was my first full-time teaching job I was often grateful for his support and for the way he cut through or ignored thorny issues, though for my entire teaching career I could not mark up a set of papers in fewer than six or seven hours, sometimes more, and never chose to learn how. The problems in a student paper intrigued me. The lives of the students, who would otherwise repeat their errors throughout their academic lives, throughout their lives, kept me diligent. Was the director of the program advising something that would undermine their prose style forever? A disastrous prospect. My colleagues, when I told them my theories, thought I was either being pretentious or just too dumb to work more quickly, and they may well have been right. I had a lot of theories in those days, as so many teachers do when they start. After twenty years of sleepwalking in classrooms, I had quite fallen in love with literature and with its words, and my colleagues—who had not hated school—were better schooled, more sensible and balanced, comfortably wiser. Often enough I would see them smile too knowingly when I began to pontificate.

Michigan, sheltered from the world, simmering in the great words, had allowed me to search vigorously among the twenty-odd men in myself for the one I was and wanted to be, and books had been my hinge. That day in Ann Arbor when I had stepped into a classroom as teacher, and all the days that followed, I knew I had found one of the people I was meant to be, however late, but not too late. I felt a power I did not know I had, and shock that it was, after so many years of hating and fearing and being bored by classrooms, I discovered that they could be magical places in which momentous events occurred. I became guardian and guide for all of the remarkable novels, essays, poems, and stories that had themselves begun to change my life, fill me with words and images and understanding.

In front of a class, tugged, made electrically alive by the presence of students, I found that my chronic shyness, my diffidence, every recalcitrant atom of my brain dissolved, and, almost disembodied, my voice took flight. I did not know I knew so much. I did not know I knew so little. All of my senses were sharper. I was sometimes in a state of near ecstasy. The mumbler became silver-tongued Saint John Chrysostom, the "honey-mouthed." Ahab, Hester, Hamlet, Huck, Tess, Nick Adams, Joseph K. and Gregor Samsa, Crazy Jane and Hotspur and Falstaff and scores of others who had lived in me, in the marrow of my bones, from the moment I'd met them, leaped out, grew wings, soared for a moment. I *was* Heathcliff.

I once became Ahab, began stomping around with my noisy peg leg, stood up on the top of the desk and declaimed that this was what they had shipped for, and left the class-room puffed as a peacock. We had a family dinner in a local Szechuan Taste restaurant that night and while we were shar-ing the chicken chow fun I heard the words "Moby Dick" from an adjacent table behind me. It was one of my best stu-dents and I reached back and touched her arm gently after she indicated that she was talking about a certain ass who thought he was Ahab, so she would wait to finish her story until after we left.

I see now many years later, and quite clearly as I did not see then, that I did not have a great or original mind for litera-ture. My only academic gift—a minor, narrow one—was a flair for taking this literature I loved, which I knew had transformed my life and might transform other lives, and sharing it enthusi-astically with others. A few bush-league theories sometimes blinded me, too often I played the buffoon, but mostly what I brought was unalloyed enthusiasm.

I had my days. And I won't be shy of it: sometimes some-thing caught fire in my lungs and words I did know were there swept free, coupled with long quotations I did not know I knew. In students I loved most the spark of wit, the abrupt challenge, the maverick mind, the kid who grew, the antique lady who could not have had much time left to use the ideas and skills she craved, the dullard whose life was electrically changed not by me but by reading "The Metamorphosis," which I had only assigned.

At times I saw myself as a ham with an itch to be public

"like a frog," like a shill. Melville scraped that big, joyous, mysterious, terrifying book off the underside of his brain, and I dared to prattle on about it, play Ahab? I also disliked many of the "learned, respectable bald heads" I met in the academy, colleagues who had nothing of the Great Song in them, not the rawness and restlessness anywhere of life, nor any feeling for students other than that they were the enemy, to be feared, to be held in contempt—the martinet: he who flunked all but one student in a class of twenty-seven, to "uphold standards"; one who never let students speak because they "had so little, really, to say"; he who never held conferences; high fliers who wanted to "hit the bastards with poetry," "subvert them with metaphor," "wire them into Whitman"; teachers who shouldn't be teaching, teaching students who shouldn't be students, remedial students for whom there might be no remedy.

I knew I could be kind and, when appropriate, encouraging. After I had worked in publishing, my judgment became surer. One shy student asked in a writing course if she could give me a longer manuscript. I thought it a compelling short book on cats passing through her hands and life and then dying in New York's Animal Medical Center. It needed little work, I sent her to an editor who specialized in books about animals, and *A Snowflake in My Hand* is still in print more than thirty-five years later. I had given its author, Samantha Mooney, a B in an earlier literature class. I changed that grade, a year after the class ended; I made it an A, the only time I changed a grade with no justification other than that I selfishly didn't want to think I'd given such a fine writer less. The dean called me down, raised his voice, wondered if I was having an affair with her, said this wasn't done, but let it stand.

I taught for nearly thirty years, first by day in the Bronx, then by necessity in the night session on Park Avenue when I became a book editor. Toward the end, I felt less sure that what I could tell anyone was of crucial importance to them. I was tired. I had begun to cheat in small ways—finally saying less in the borders of a student's paper, repeating myself, waffling generally. I had always said I would quit when that happened.

I was restless, too. The classroom suddenly felt safe, and I wanted to live closer to risk. And I wanted to be more private. I worried that my late-arriving love of the classroom had seduced me away from others of the people I had found in my shape shift. I had spent too much time in the tenured safety of schools, I argued to myself; I wanted to do and say things that had chilled me when I talked about them in class or read them in books. If I could, I wanted to live in the tumultuous "outside" world—fraught with danger—that I had tried for so many years to prepare students to live in.

Leonard was the image of he whom I wanted not to become and might be sliding toward.

And there was something else: years earlier, after three years at Hunter, with a wife and four small children to support, idealism bent to necessity. I could think of no alternative than to apply for a second job. I had to ask the provost of the college for this honor and he gave it, with the caveat that my teaching not suffer and that I speak with him again in a few years; meanwhile, I had his permission. So I had myself transferred to the main branch of Hunter College, at Park Avenue and Sixty-ninth Street, into the night session, where the diversity of the students was immense: one businessman converted to scholar and went on for a PhD in American literature and a distinguished career at Vassar; several had jobs in publishing; one tough (who threatened to kill a young colleague) later made an appearance in the

Post for having murdered a neighbor; some were intense, some were there for an evening snooze. I think I preferred all this without hesitation to the more homogenized day students.

Periodically I had to argue with a dean or provost that my publishing life had in fact made me a more effective teacher, that I could now advise students—especially in practical literary matters—out of experience. I knew exactly how a manuscript traveled from a typewriter to a publishing house, and how it became a book. I knew what an editor did and had begun to do this myself, and with a great new passion. Several chairs warned me that editing could not possibly have improved my teaching. One noted that my obvious commercialism and the fact that I had begun to write amusing stories about fly-fishing were in fact embarrassments to the English Department, though one chair later invited me to prepare a grand proposal for a course on book publishing, which I did and later taught—and the department received a hefty grant for this.

They did not know and I told no one that for four or five years I also ghostwrote books. Four of them. One a best seller. All written after a full day in publishing, a full evening at the college, each in five or six weeks. One of my sons remembers going to bed with the sound of the typewriter and waking to the same machine-gun tattoo, for years. I learned from each, swore finally that I would never do another, and marveled that I had survived. Sometime in those years I read Roth's *Letting Go* and liked it, though less so than later Roth. I thought of writing a book called *Holding*.

Through all these years I taught hard, went to all department meetings, and took some role in the complex political problems, sometimes concerning changes in the canon, sometimes concerning who would be fired or hired, at time adjustments of standards, which most of the department thought had headed south—so that one of the old guard once remarked that he could remember when more than half of his students were literate.

For years there were reports at the meetings about a teacher in the English Department who had not received tenure nor been reappointed and who then sued the college. The case had become as tangled as *Jarndyce v. Jarndyce* in *Bleak House* and lasted almost as long. Then, a few years before I retired I was asked to chair what was to be absolutely the last, the final hearing on the matter.

The facts sounded simple: Hoddeson had been hired to put the very sloppy freshman composition program in order. He had been a writer for *Barron's* and he had explicit letters advising him that he need not publish, long a requirement for tenure and promotion in most American colleges. So he didn't write academic papers but did, after four years, put the program in very solid order—and then he was warned by the same chair who had hired him that he would not be rehired at the end of the academic year because he had not published. So he sued and the union kept his case alive for a short time and then went on to what they considered more worthy causes. Hoddeson hung on to the case like a mongoose, and each year the matter came up, was discussed, was delayed, was turned down, was kept alive on the man's shrewd appeals.

So I convened the meeting and three of us talked, split hairs, grew quiet, then loud, ate our academic pie, and in the end thoroughly analyzed the long document Hoddeson had prepared—brilliantly, I thought, with all of the letters reproduced—and voted two to one to grant tenure. The dissenting vote insisted that even though Hoddeson had been told in writing by the chair of the English Department that he would not need to publish, he should have known that he did.

Three months later I was told that Donna Shalala, then president of Hunter, had convened her own council of presidents of all the sister colleges and they had voted unanimously not to give the man tenure, a decision for which there was finally no further appeal.

After twenty-eight years in the classroom, which I had loved deeply, I abruptly retired and accelerated my commitment to book publishing, and a business world I had begun to find cleaner, and I became a full-fledged full-time minuscule but independent book publisher.

One day Leonard, my old department head, then university president, called me at my office and asked if we could have lunch. We had not spoken or exchanged a letter in more than twenty-six years—and I was oddly anxious to see who he was, what he had become. I am addicted to such reunions—to see the arc of the story. For a moment, I wondered wildly if he wanted to propose a book to me or invite me back to academia as a chair or provost or dean. A novel of his would be the worst; I worried on my way to the nearby Bavarian restaurant that I might have to read about characters in a college that was not Harvard.

But I needn't have worried. He'd merely been offered, as a sinecure, the happy and easy task, he thought, of establishing a publishing house for the city colleges.

Not quite so easy, I told him, and then enumerated forty or fifty skills he would have to learn, as I had, before he could make sensible decisions. I did this very slowly so he could write it all down on his notepad. As an afterthought, I asked if he had done any editing. Only freshman compositions.

When I was satisfied that I had in good conscience not allowed his sinecure to go unexamined, I asked how he had gotten on with Donna Shalala and he said he had once done her a great favor and that they had gotten along beautifully after that. Only mildly interested, I asked him what that was. "Just a favor," he said. "There was a tenure case and hundreds of pages to read, and she asked me not to read any of it." I said nothing and he added, "She just wanted me to vote her way, and I did. It looked pretty complicated and I was busy. I think there was a lot of back pay involved."

Plans for the new press were soon abandoned and I never saw Leonard again—though I think of him now and then, and of my first days in the classroom, and all the immense vitality I felt then and my grave doubts that I had made too much of myself in the classroom and had not been nearly wise enough for the students. But then, even now, in my eighties, several times a year, some middle-aged man or woman whose face is foreign to me comes to my table in a restaurant on the Upper West Side or meets me on Broadway, and despite my weight and wrinkles says, "You're Professor Lyons. Many years ago, you changed my life."

9

ROSE

I did not think seriously about my mother until she died. If you're lucky, death finally allows you to see the story whole, though that rarely happens.

We had had no wars. From my early teens I had managed to keep her at a safe remove. Cézanne had wanted to avoid anyone's "grapplings" digging into him and I wanted to avoid any with which my mother might try to snare me. I had trouble enough holding myself in tow. Perhaps I felt, near the end, that she would lean on me for money, emotional coin, something, but she died first. Perhaps the three years I spent in the boarding school had hardened my heart; I cannot remember feeling much I could call affection after I left the Burt School, when she married Arthur Lyons.

There are photographs of her on my grandparents' farm near Liberty, New York, standing with her three brothers and older sister, all in rustic clothing, serious and stiff, my mother the youngest in that family of Russian immigrants who had fled Pinsk when the czar needed more fodder for one of his wars. Her father, a butcher, had brought his wife and two children to the Lower East Side, helped found the Pinsk temple, and then gone upstate to raise chickens; later, with an old-country friend from Pinsk who specialized in laundry, he bought the old run-down Laurel House Hotel that sat majestically at the head of Kaaterskill Falls. There are photographs of my mother at the hotel, smiling, kicking up a leg in a country dance, often with a crowd of friends and relatives around, for she always enjoyed a crowd. She always appeared in such high spirits in these photos—a full-blown smile on her mouth and in her eyes, often dancing, full of vitality and joy, with a kind of happy openness to the whole business of living, to the vast mystery and adventure that might yet come. She had an infectious warmth, an abandon, a delight in who she was and who she would someday be. And there is another photograph of her with my father, before or after they married I cannot tell, that I found in a sealed envelope among her papers on the day her death was discovered. It was a posed shot, he in one of those funny old swimsuits with a top like a tank top, with stripes, my mother in a loose skirt and blouse, my father hamming, my mother trying to suppress too much fun in the matter. The photograph, in sepia, had faded slightly but was not wrinkled or creased like the others she kept in a big round box. A piece of firm cardboard had been cut carefully to size and placed in the envelope with the photograph so it would not bend. My father had dark curly hair, like me, and an ample mouth. His face and body were taut, and I remember having heard that, though small, he had been an excellent athlete. He ran a little insurance brokerage, Nat Ress, Inc., but made important extra money as a kind of junk dealer, buying up small estates, taking an end table or a secretary for his apartment, selling most of it off quick, for the short money. I always wanted to know more about the man, much more, and still know little because I never once asked my mother and then because of several events that took place after she died. At times the mystery of his life and death, and their love, was so palpable that I thought I must be a bastard, or that there had never been such a person as Nat Ress, or that he was still alive but had committed a great crime that all the relatives in both families were hiding. What is left of the two families, one Russian, the other Ukrainian, know nothing of each other; none now alive are old enough to have known my father, to have gone to my parents' wedding. One cousin, now dead, was seven when my father died, and she remembered, at a long lunch, enough about Nat Ress's death to make him alive to me; but I had a busy life and when I finally found time for a second meeting, she had died—I had waited too long. What I have gathered is that the Resses, a generation back, had been reasonably successful coffee merchants, had probably lost most of their money in the 1929 crash, and had a certain reserve I didn't see in the Bernsteins. The Resses were professional people. My mother's parents spoke Yiddish and only broken English, and her brothers laughed loudly and told stories partly in English, with punch lines in Yiddish. Her oldest brother stole an insurance settlement from the family and then vanished for several years, returning, after World War One, gassed and tamed. One married a showgirl, another a blond four inches taller than he was, after years of girl chasing.

Different as the families were, it must have been hard to resist Rose. She was too warm and full of genuine smiles and she was innocent. She had loose soft hair, and freckles, and from her dancing she was light on her feet. She must have reminded the Resses of a hummingbird—always in motion, never obtrusive. She loved them because they were his family and because she loved almost everyone who did not bite her. Even later, much later, when people did bite her, a part of her always wanted a table of people to love each other, to be full of stories together, full of laughter, who believed there was surely a way to keep the world aflame with smiles.

In the photograph of the two my mother is looking at my father with what could only be called deep affection. They were both full of affection, celebrating the fact of love, the delight in each other, the established delirium, the promise of a life that would later narrow so abruptly in its options for her, so that she became a person waiting to endure whatever would happen to her next. With him, in this photograph, she was a young woman full of energy and hope.

This was the first photograph I had seen of the man and I saw another thirty-five years later, given to me by a cousin. In this my parents are standing together, brightly dressed, my father with sporty brown-and-white shoes, both smiling again, the two at the time of the photographs never closer. How I would have liked to have known my father. I longed for him—for someone with whom I could talk, get counsel from, bounce against, find authority in, never authoritarianism. Arthur had been bland, stupidly bossy, unavailable. The hunger was so great that once, when I had given my friend Schmulke a check for a poker loss, he called and asked for my father's name. My checks then carried my full name, Nathan Ress Lyons. His father had known a Nat Ress well. I raced from my house, ran thirty blocks in high gear, and the mild man could only tell me that Nat had been his best friend, a nice guy, and a great handball player. My questions drew only a few more generalities. How I would have loved to have known my mother then. I was not there, of course, so I have had to imagine, dozens of times, piecing together stories I later learned from a cousin, how it was eighty-seven years ago: the grisly night in March, my mother six months pregnant, her worry that the slight inflection in her voice, just for a moment, had been too insistent. The rain ferocious, without letup all afternoon, mixed with sleet, sending the last remnants of snow into dirty little rivers at the curb. My father in the three-room apartment in Bensonhurst for two days then, coughing a deep raspy cough that drew sharp pains in his chest, that he said did not hurt a bit, smiling. My mother changing her mind: they would not go to the party. It was all right. Everyone would understand. They had been living in the cocoon of their new life, thinking of their first child; they had not been nearly as social as they both liked. The tone, the very slight insistence in her words, was an idle sound, quick off her tongue, and she regretted it. So she said: "Don't let's go, Nat. Please let's not." But my father—I have inherited his fatal flaw—always wanted to please and just smiled and put on his coat, and then my mother's, and they walked the nine blocks into the wet Brooklyn night to the happy gathering. He had what my cousin Lois later called a good heart. Everyone said so.

When they came back at nine-thirty he could not stop coughing. The cough was deeper in his chest and he could not stop all that night. The next day, a Monday, his fever rose to 105 degrees. His brother, Kalman, came at four and took him to the Brooklyn Jewish Hospital. He did not allow my mother to visit and for three days she begged two of her sisters-in-law to be taken there. She needed to be with him. He needed her. She felt the first tinges of something . . . had she caused this? But Mary and Jeanne, Nat's sisters, would not hear of it. It was too dangerous. Pregnant, it could be especially dangerous. So she stayed with the women in the small apartment most of Tuesday and Wednesday and then Thursday. There was no news. Or if there was news, no one would tell her. She tried to read. She fingered the edges of several magazines, could not remember the articles she had just looked at. The women made a bowl of chicken and lentil soup and begged her to eat some. She had not slept and felt faint. Then late Thursday evening, Kalman came to the apartment, took off his glasses, rubbed them clean with a white handkerchief. He loved Nat. Nat, his younger brother, had always been his best friend. Then, without looking up, he told her: "We've lost him."

She was struck dumb. It was not possible.

"Noooo," she said, her voice husky and low, a moan really.

Twenty minutes later she began to wail and sob, her sounds fierce, like those of an animal with its paw in a trap, when the pain is too sharp and there is nothing left to be done. They were terrified for her health. Her sobbing grew to be great gasps for air, a heavy heaving of her chest. Then, with their arms around her, and because you cannot sob forever, she grew silent and they could only hear the sound of her breathing, and they were all terrified for her and for the baby, and for her unending grief.

She did not smile those last days of March 1932, nor in April or May, and during the first day or so of June those around her, and her doctor, were convinced that she would die of grief if not childbirth. No one could survive such grief. Her breathing was heavy and anguished. And she had caused all this, she thought; it was that slight inflection in her voice when she first wanted to go out that wet night in March, a lifetime ago, the edge, the longing, the stupidity she could not erase: her own hand had struck him down.

Her doctor said that she must be prepared to lose the child. He told her sisters-in-law that her hysteria gave her little chance of delivering the child safely. Late May and the first few days of June were heavy and hot that spring and she lay moaning on a sofa in the little apartment, a fan aimed at her face, making low guttural sounds, sweating profusely even as her older sister, Rae, and her sisters-in law, and one of her nieces put cold towels on her forehead. What to do? There was no consoling her.

The relatives, to quiet her, never mentioned Nat, took away all photographs of him. Did they want to destroy all evidence that Nat Ress had ever existed? And what they missed my stepfather got, or my half sister, much later.

On June 2, the doctor said that there was just no chance of saving the child and that there was only a slight chance of saving her. She was frozen, hyperventilating.

Late on June 4, Jeanne's husband took Rose to the hospital, the same hospital where, three months earlier, Nat had died of pneumonia. None of them smiled. Rose was delirious.

And then, at two the next morning, she went into the final stages of labor. No one had any faith that Mama would survive, or that I would, but they elected to save her—which would have been my decision too—but survive we both did, and I got my father's name, perhaps to take his place, but from birth was called Nicki.

ONE DAY, AFTER I had been married for four years, my mother phoned me in Ann Arbor and, her voice breaking, told me that she and Arthur were to be divorced. "You knew," she said, her voice barely audible. "You must have known how bad it was . . . all those years." They had been married nineteen years. Mama was now nearly sixty.

No, I had not known. I had thought all marriages were like that—cold, full of quibbles and shouts, with one person pressing a thumb down steadily, in the name of reason and what was thought to be invariably good sense. I had vowed to build mine inversely.

"Don't hate him," she said, crying openly now. "It was wrong, Nicki. It was wrong from the start."

And so my mother took a second swift blow to the kidneys—or had already taken many more: the first husband, the one she had married in the full bloom of love, dead abruptly, and now the second, who had married her during the Depression to get Nat Ress, Inc., wanted to marry the widow of a fellow who had been president of a vastly larger insurance firm. Much later, Arthur told me he had to do this before it was too late; he also said he had paid for Rose's teeth. She had been duped when she married him and cheated of the real stuff for nearly twenty years thereafter.

And so one circle had closed, or at least the arc had turned another notch downward, and the event was yet another blow to that bright young woman in the photographs, off the farm and with a great readiness for life—brimming with love.

Sometime after Nat died she had moved in with her parents on Walton Avenue in the Bronx, and she had tried to make Nat Ress, Inc. work. Her brothers Dave and Jack—bachelors in their forties—lived there, too, and I barely remember her in those years except for visits during the summers at the Laurel House. Mostly, I remember my grandfather, a great patriarch of a man, a massively silent presence in my life, smelling from the salves he used on his legs for gout and edema, reading his *Forward* in a corner rocking chair, never once in my presence raising his voice, commanding the Seders and smiling when I found the *afikomen*. Then, soon after my fifth birthday, my mother installed me in Burt's. Years later cousins told me that my uncles said I was being spoiled rotten by grandparents.

I stayed at the school for three very long years and might not have thought it so brutal were it not for the ferocious tension which continued long after she married and we moved to a small house in Mount Vernon with her new husband.

WHEN I TRY to think of my mother during all those years, during the war when we lived in Mount Vernon and then in Brooklyn, and even into my years in college and then the Army, I have great trouble seeing her as more than a shadow. A certain sadness may have come into her—a kind of bourgeois dullness and resignation. She put on weight. She dressed in suits. She never once contradicted her new husband. She had frequent mah-jongg games. She got a live-in housekeeper. She arranged parties to which a dozen relatives came. She kept a clean house. She cooked. She dutifully went with her husband and their daughter, Amie, and me to visit his family in Bushwick—his old father who had been a fishmonger with a cart, his warm mother and quiet, spinster Aunt Kitty—dull days. At one of Mama's parties, Arthur flagrantly fondled Neale Elish's breasts and I know Mama saw and merely smiled wanly.

Meals were mostly silent, with Mama preparing and serving the food, saying little—I cannot once remember her initiating a conversation. They were vaguely Democrats, mostly bound to the immediate and the palpable. They rarely argued. Arthur's view was the only view; I cannot remember her standing up once and when an argument was with me I never appealed to her for a second opinion. Now and again she suggested I read a book—C. S. Forester, perhaps—but I read only what was assigned in class, and as little of that as I could get away with. I broke away from the house whenever I could, to fish at Sheepshead Bay or in upstate New York—and I began to play basketball with great ferocity, though I was small for my age and a year ahead in school.

By high school, Mama told me several times, I never whistled anymore and I guess some of the inertia and sadness—the profound weariness of life in the house on East Twenty-fourth Street in Brooklyn—crept into my bones.

Mama rarely nagged me in my teens but she nagged Amie. After I had turned quietly and walked off, she stopped biting me. I had little enough to do with my sister, ten years younger, and kept trying to get by, not fighting resignation to a bourgeois fate, not embracing it, wondering vaguely what sustained a marriage like my mother's, how I could free myself. Beer and basketball helped me at Penn and then, suddenly, I was away, in the Army, in France.

She told me how, when it was ending with Arthur, he would come back at one or two in the morning, to keep residence, to get a better deal after he ended it, and how he demanded that she wash his socks, which she did.

Even during the years after her divorce, when I struggled to keep my large family afloat, I saw little enough of Mama. We visited for Thanksgiving dinner, for two or three other meals a year. She was kind to my four children, had no idea what to say to my wife, took a secretarial job to increase her Social Security benefits, then volunteered at a thrift shop, read a best seller or two now and then, played mah-jongg once a week, found a few friends in the East Side building in which she had an L-shaped studio apartment. Once, in our apartment, she came into the living room and said quietly that there was a problem in the kitchen. It didn't sound important but when I got there the curtain near the open window was ablaze and the fire spread to the heavily repainted walls and ceiling before it was doused. Sometimes her words trailed off, drifted; I once asked if there was something I could do for her and she said, "I just need a kind word now and then." She didn't get one from me and she didn't get any from Amie. I was teaching at Hunter then, no more than three blocks away, but never visited her by myself, only with my family, when invited. Once, when she stayed with us at the summer cabin we had taken in Woodstock and we were busy with four small children for several days, she began to cry and Mari told me in a whisper that I should tell my mother I loved her and I could not.

And then one morning in March, in her seventy-fourth year, a friend of hers called me and said, "Your mother is dead."

AT FIRST I was sure that she had died that night, a Saturday, perhaps Friday. But the superintendent at her apartment building said that he had not seen her since nine on Monday evening, when she brought him a peach pie she had baked, so at least it happened after that. Mama was always baking peach pies for someone. Based on the position in which the police found her—a friend of hers had called them about noon when she did not show for a brunch date, then me—her death had to have been an abrupt cessation of the heart, which they say is a blessing.

I sat in her warm little apartment for an hour—not sad but light-headed, my body mostly elsewhere, my chest heavy. At first the super was there with the four policemen, and there was barely room to turn in the small room, with the cops milling around, poking into drawers, touching the china, touching Mama's last-worn cotton blouse on the back of the chair. Several walked to the door of the bathroom, looked, then walked away. Then all of them except a rookie left, and he sat down in Mama's armchair, his face a pocked white stone, and I sat on the gold velour couch in the living room corner of the L-shaped room, neither of us having much to say to the other.

"You're the son?" he asked me after a long silence.

I nodded.

"Anyone else in the family?"

I mentioned my wife, four children. Then, remembering, and remembering that I should call her: "Amie, my kid sister." She was divorced and lived alone in the East Thirties.

"That's good," he said, tightening his lips, nodding. "Big family. It don't hurt so much then."

Ten minutes later he said: "The M.E. should be here any-time now. Then we can wrap this up for you." It was a Sunday in mid-March, late morning, raining, the rain in Mama's court-yard locking us in that much tighter, her small world made smaller by the closed door.

I walked around this little apartment in which I had spent no more than a couple of dozen Sunday and holiday afternoons in the more than a decade Mama had lived here, since the divorce, since she sold the Brooklyn house. Why hadn't I man-aged any time alone with this old woman of whom I had always been wary, who I knew so slenderly?

There were a few pieces of fine old furniture, the residue of early years: the great oak dining table that had belonged to my grandparents, which I remembered from their apartment in the Bronx from Seders; the walnut end tables and the match-ing secretary. The dining chairs, oak like the table but of mod-ern vintage, with shiny black plastic seat covers. The drapes and rug were gray, and they made the little room smaller, drearier. The blanket had been pulled off Mama's bed for some reason; the bed was in the alcove and it doubled as a second couch, and the bathroom door, to its left, was half open. That's where she had to be. In the bathroom. There was nowhere else.

On a single black wall-shelf there were a dozen books, no more; I had given her most of them for birthdays over the past several years and a few I remembered from the house in Brooklyn. A *Ladies' Home Journal*, a *Vogue*, and a *New York Post* lay on the glass coffee table, neatly arranged, as in a doctor's office. Amie had given her the new color television set that I knew she watched until one or two each morning, sometimes later. Mama increasingly had trouble getting to sleep and even with pills rarely stopped watching or pacing until well after midnight. On her night table were six or seven plastic pill vials, yellowish, with white caps. I had sometimes thought of her here alone, half-drugged, awake and walking back and forth in the prison of this little gray apartment with the gold couch, when I was up, too, pacing or typing; perhaps she was thinking of her first husband, her second, her daughter, my large family; I remembered my need to finish some piece of writing that would pay down the mounting dung heap of debt. Her three brothers and sister had died and she had only seen two of their children in the ensuing years, though she had always tried to hold together her family, keep connections. Still, everyone drifted into their own worlds; for a gregarious tribe, the Bernsteins were oddly allergic to phones and letter writing. Neither of us had seen any of the Resses since I was thirteen.

Most of Mama's friends from the boisterous days at Laurel House were dead. Her three or four new friends were older women without men who happened to live in the building. They had hard, humorless faces; the gray business of their lives had gone through them, coloring everything gray; they talked mostly about Minnie's kidney and Paula's gallbladder, and about Miami Beach and grandchildren. They played mah-jongg and canasta together. "Are you wearing a brassiere yet, darling?" one of them had asked my daughter, then twelve.

Near the secretary was the etching by Jozef Israëls that her old suitor Jesse W. Eric had given her; it was of an aged peasant woman in a shawl, sitting swaybacked before a fireplace, hands extended. I had often seen her looking at it, a sad smile on her face. The secretary held all of her papers, neatly filed so that her affairs would cause no one undue difficulty later. She had thought about the end; she concerned herself with Amie and me and everyone else so much, I imagined that there was no concern left for herself. I riffled through the most conspicuous papers, knowing I would later have to look at them all closely. I found no notes to herself, no diary, no words. I had faintly hoped that there might be love letters, any letters from my father, any evidence of him, his death certificate, some other document. Nothing that I could find, though I did not look at it all. There would be time for that. I remembered Arthur demanding that I never mention that other man, and he was never mentioned, and I was quite sure Arthur had insisted that Rose rid herself of any such records of the man. I found my grandfather's naturalization papers, awarded twenty years after he came from Pinsk; I found Mama's rabbinical decree of divorce from Arthur. There were the many decks of cards, several of them opened, three lapsed insurance policies, an old lease, a notebook listing the few contents of her safe deposit box, keys, blank notepads, empty envelopes, sharpened pencils, a *Playbill* for *Gypsy*, a stack of Amie's report cards from high school. It was all neatly arranged. She had simplified, simplified; she had eliminated all but the husk of her life.

In the closet I found the mink coat Mama had bought at the thrift shop where she volunteered. It had cost a few hundred dollars, a raggedy old hunk of mink, not full-length, worn hard. She once told me that if she was going to die poor—her greatest fear—she would rather do so in mink. On the shelf above the clothes in her closet I found the old round hatbox in which I knew she had for decades kept the family photographs and I took it down and began to sift through the old pictures: faded ochre and sepia prints from before I was born; starchly posed shots of my maternal grandparents, Louis and Ida; pictures of my uncles and aunts and cousins, dozens of them, at various moments in their lives; pictures of the Laurel House, our home in Mount Vernon, the stucco two-family house in Brooklyn; baby pictures, only a few posed, some in sandboxes or on someone's knee; pictures of Amie and of my children. And there were those pictures of Mama at the farm, and later, in some dance position, with one skinny leg extended out and up and high. She loved to dance, had once—so a few uncles said—even been on the stage, though I never knew which or where. There were pictures of thirty or forty young adults, friends of Mama's with Mama among them, at the hotel near Kaaterskill Falls, arms around each other, laughing at the world, funny in those old bloomerlike clothes, hamming it up. Always, in those faded pictures, my mother had animation and expectation in her face, a capacity for fun, an unselfconsciousness; she was what anyone would call pretty, with loose soft hair, an impish turning up of her lips, wide eyes, a flair for life.

The pictures I found of me showed a boy now plump, now narrow, toad and fox, now dressed for some party or at the beach or playing basketball, or just returned from a fishing trip. Looking at my face—at four or seven or thirteen or twenty—I tried to read the expressions and could not tell who was behind those eyes that looked out at me from so many years earlier.

My cheeks turned red from embarrassment.

I had not known my mother in the faintest degree and now she was gone. All I knew of her was inextricably bound to me and my life, and I had not the slightest idea what the sum of all those faces in the hatbox could be. If what was in this little L-shaped room was all I'd ever know now of my mother, after all those years of not caring who she was, I was quite sure I'd never know anything.

THE AFTERNOON LIMPED along and I looked at the old prints with sharp creases, wrinkles, bent corners, with bits missing, smudges, fingerprints, faded sections, vanished sections— while I waited for the medical examiner to come and pronounce Mama dead and tell me what physiological thing had finally finished the long journey for her, and I kept thinking that maybe, perhaps in the battered old hatbox, among the old family pictures, there was a message for me. I had been looking for a message all that year. I was on sabbatical from teaching. I had had nearly a full year with only my second job, at Crown, and I had been ransacking the basement of my soul for some message. Now it was March and I was more exhausted than when I'd held three jobs simultaneously, when I was editing at Crown, teaching at Hunter, doing ghostwriting and other writing, but I had done no work of my own, found no messages. I was tired to the bone, of more than ten years of being a dray horse in a ring and urging myself to move faster. I had not thought it could happen again, that numbness I'd felt when I lived alone, the weight of all that soul thrashing and doubt like a great lump on my back, my life listless, sour. I loved my family and I thought I had left all that.

Looking at the pictures, I felt my brain suddenly become ferociously active, as if shot through, awakened, with a burst of electricity. The old photographs reached out to me, swarmed in my head, fathered whole events. But the recollections were piecemeal, without order, sometimes blurred, sometimes diamond-sharp, memories I had locked away a hundred years earlier, not to be thought of again, concerning events I had full forgotten, that now wanted out.

THEY HAD LEFT Mama in the position in which she had died. I glimpsed her, sitting there, when I first went to the telephone, and then avoided looking each time that unending afternoon when the one phone rang on the night table near her bed, in front of the bathroom. I called my wife a second time and then my half-sister Amie. A friend or two of Mama's called. I called Amie once more. Amie called me—"What's taking so long?"— and I called her again, much later. Mama had surely died as suddenly as you could die, a blessing.

A tall captain of the police came in with two men about three o'clock, looked around, asked the rookie who was in charge, and then began to root around like a carrion crow, pecking in different corners of the room, tossing papers from the secretary onto the bed, fussing in her closets, bureau drawers, my mother's purse. He carried himself upright and with authority and never once spoke to me and it was not until an hour later that I realized he had taken a small cache of my mother's stuff and that he had given me neither his name nor a receipt. Why hadn't I protested? This was my first death. There was that. My head spun and I had sunk into myself, into the box of old photographs; I might have grasped the reins of my life, or thought I had, but I still allowed the world to happen to me. I asked the young cop and he said that I'd get it all back of course—the purse, whatever papers the captain had removed. Three months later the precinct didn't know what I was talking about, didn't know of such a captain. They had nothing, had heard nothing. I was thick with work then. Along with the purse and whatever was in it, I have no idea what else was gone.

EACH TIME I came back from the telephone that long afternoon, I would sit in my corner of the gold couch and, after a few moments, begin to study the photographs again. My children had liked to take them out and spread them on the rug and look and point and laugh and ask questions. There was no chronology, no order. They were jumbled together, some faded, some clear, some sixty or seventy years old, some of my children, Mama's grandchildren, mixed with the old ones, frozen moments, scattered, disorderly, not an accurate view of anyone or any time, but all that remained. I did not feel myself a part of the life seeping from the prints at first, then, as the images begat other more fluid, moving, images in my mind, as I sorted through them in some nagging urgency to make sense of them all, some meaning of them, I found the racing of my mind slow and slow again, just as I once had to slow down my life, which had been slipping steadily, inexorably, through my hands. I had not been able to control it once. I had been rigged up, like a puppet, playing a role that had been written out for me, a hostage to an alien script.

Hadn't there been something small and mysterious, like a small flame in damp straw, hidden inside me? I had scarcely known how to fan it forth. And why? For what reasons? I had always done what I had to do, little more. I did what I was told. I smiled when I was supposed to smile. I tried desperately to find a way to remove those bands from my chest, that extraordinary, constant, unyielding pressure. I kept looking at the little curly-haired boy in those photographs, now one, now four or five, now almost in his teens. There were even some of a bar mitzvah party in our backyard, which I remembered too well. And scattered throughout there were those photographs of Mama, a teenager on the farm in Liberty, at the Laurel House, in large groups, with me alone, and then with Amie or Arthur, aging before my eyes, pressing toward this day and me sitting in her neat little room with the rookie, and she there too.

I looked at the photographs and they were a part of some drama I could not quite understand, scattered and inchoate, and they were a part of me and not a part of me and I tried to let them come closer but I still had a passive center, a place that could let an arrogant police captain swipe some of my mother's few possessions and say nothing, do nothing. By seven the medical examiner had still not come. "He'll come," said the young policeman when I asked if we should call a third time. "I bet they only got one M.E. on duty for the whole county of Manhattan on Sunday."

I called Amie again. She said, "She's still there. Still in the bathroom? Goddamn those bastards." I told her I had called the funeral home and the lawyer. I wanted her to know everything I was doing.

The funeral parlor called and asked whether I was Orthodox. I said I wasn't. "Then you want embalming?" the voice asked. He said they could ice the remains but since the funeral would not be until Wednesday, earliest, I should choose embalming. Saying the word made me wince. The light at the windows had faded a few hours earlier and I sat there in the darkening room, the young policeman and I, silent, and then I turned on two of the lamps. Even then the room was dark, shadowed, so I tried the ceiling light. It was too bright. I was tired. I had tried to write all the necessary notes to myself on a little piece of folded paper. Her Social Security number. The building superintendent's phone number. Numbers and names: of friends and relatives to be called. The number of her safe deposit box—for which, in a small spiral notebook, she had listed its simple contents. Her phone book identified her son and daughter, the doctor she used, and even the local precinct; I took down the latter number, which I knew would be valuable when I tried to retrieve the purse and whatever other items the police captain had taken. Mama had not raged against the dying of the light but welcomed it.

About seven, I caught the faintest odor—delicate and thin at first, not fresh but not unpleasant. I thought someone might be cooking an exotic food, perhaps the superintendent's wife, next door.

"Mind if I open the back door, sir?" my companion asked. No. I did not mind. He opened it and there was a rush of cold March air. It was still raining and I could hear the wet sounds of rain falling on the pavement of Mama's terrace, see the glints of light on the puddles.

I went over to the ceiling light switch and turned on the main light now. They were still too bright and I felt dislocated. I saw the apartment in all of its smallness, its confinement, too clearly. "My little world," Mama used to say, spreading her arms, looking around the L-shaped room. Ten years ago, when'd she first moved in, she had brought in a decorator, gotten those gray drapes specially made, bought the gold velour couch, fitted the little place with what would fit of her old furniture.

On the bed, where the cops had thrown most of her papers, I saw a couple of the many fishing books I had written, my collection of Jones Very's poems, my essay refuting Saint Augustine's critique of literature as immoral and another essay distinguishing between the spiritual love of Perceval and the worldly love of Lancelot in Chrétien de Troyes, and, in the little pile, my article on Thomas Nashe's prose style, one on Kafka and Poe, copies of *Field & Stream* and the *Yale Review* and the *New York Times*. A strange stew—less eclectic than schizophrenic, erratic. Had I sent them all to her? I couldn't remember having done so and wondered why I had. She was proud of them nevertheless and always very serious when she introduced me to her friends as her son, Dr. Nathan Ress Lyons, the professor.

What Mama gathered of my strange intellectual life was probably blurred by the chaotic life we lived during those hurricane years. I was always trying to preserve something already gained, to hold on, to protect the hawk in me like Samson his hair, but blood and money had become linked. I could feel when not paying a credit card balance became dangerous. I wrote long letters to the IRS, explaining why I had not mailed in an installment as promised. I begged Chemical Bank to hold checks for just two more days—I'd pay double interest, anything—but not to bounce three checks. My near insolvency must have bewildered her. I was her son, Professor Lyons, but she would have preferred me solvent. She understood solvency better than art. But she offered no advice, no criticism. Not even when financial disaster, several times, seemed imminent, when I sold fly rods, books, everything I had to sell, feeling sometimes as if I was living off my own blood transfusions. Had she found any answers? Had she done so well? She wanted to protect me, perhaps, from her woes, her nasty war with Arthur, which she had neither wit nor strength to win. Even if it thrust her that much further into loneliness, her darkest ogre—even if her quiet little life led her further and further from the Belle of the Hotel she once had been, she could do this one thing for me: stay away.

I had read some of the best that men have thought or

written; I had taught for a dozen years and, instead of the old empty-handedness, had a dozen balls wildly rotating in the air; and my debts reached absurd proportions, increasing in some terrifying, mad geometric progression that I could not understand. The grocery store dunned me; checks bounced; a credit card company demanded that a restaurant not honor my card but take it forcibly from me, if need be, and cut it in half; and the IRS drummed on my liver, relentless as cancer. But what I remember most about all those years is the shy eager smile on Jenny's face, Jenny; Charlie taking the measure of a fat tree trunk with his eye, then climbing it by sheer will; walking to school with Tony, he holding firmly on to one of my fingers as we crossed the street, losing it, then grasping my coat pocket; Paul, when he was eight, curly-haired, teeth popping out all through the family then, being redeemed by the Tooth Fairy, who was barely solvent. I did not need photographs to remember a minute of it. I felt lonely even when only one child was away.

I FELT A blast of cold in the room, turned, and saw that the back door, which I had closed, had blown open. I closed it but ten minutes later I caught a full whiff of the odor. It was different, richer now. I had never smelled death before but there could be no mistaking it now. She must have been there for days. The odor was no longer thin and innocuous. It was a foul, pungent smell, a thick, rancid dose of which swept into my lungs, touched my brain. Out of the bathroom it had crept, from that ghostly, hooded figure there, with leg extended, slowly at first, perhaps for an hour, building upon itself, multiplying, touching everything, expanding, reaching out with its inescapable message. Now, with the terrace door closed tight, it was everywhere in the tiny room—on my skin, inside my head, in my lungs, permeating deep and quickly to the marrow of my bones. I turned my head and looked for it: it was so thick it had to be visible. I tried to breathe less deeply, to avoid it. It was everywhere, foul, sickening, and I opened the door again.

IN A POEM by Richard Eberhart, the narrator passes a ground-hog lying dead in a summer field. Even as he watches, he sees "nature ferocious in him"—maggots making a "seething caul-dron" of the thing—and the poet is filled "half with loathing, half with a strange love." He pokes it. Can his "angry stick" affect the dead thing, for good or harm? Not hardly. In autumn he returns; the "sap" is gone out of the body; only a "sodden hulk" remains. And by the next summer, there is only a little hair left, "And bones bleaching in the sunlight / Beautiful as architecture." In three years, not a sign is left. The poet, stand-ing with hand "capped" over a "withered heart," thinks, in a bold anacoluthon,

> *. . . of China and of Greece,*
> *Of Alexander in his tent;*
> *Of Montaigne in his tower,*
> *Of Saint Theresa in her wild lament.*

A single death, even that of a lowly groundhog, a Yorick

among rodents, recalls all death and then the death of those who, perhaps, defied death and, as another poet has it, "left the vivid air signed with their honour."

Sitting in that room then, that haunting poem suddenly buzzing in my ears, with the sharp March night air unable to keep the odor of death from my brain, I looked at the pile of papers the police had tossed carelessly, clumsily out of the secretary and onto the bed. The open jewel box, the missing purse. Her teeth in a glass near her bed. I looked at the great pile of family pictures from which, on that long day, so much had floated up out of forgetfulness, fit for reshaping, reborn in a dozen different configurations, like all lives, out of sequence and sync, somehow connected, not so much a continuous story as mulch, a stew. I thought of the shrouded figure in the bathroom—not my mother but her husk, hastening to return to dust.

She had looked so tired the last time I had seen her, a week earlier: shorter, stout, a little more bowlegged, tripping and stumbling now and then, burning her fingers at the stove, only her B. Altman wig trying to belie her years. "My little life," she said again—a lot of canasta, some work in the thrift shop, some visits to an abstracted son who had been in the deep glums for nearly a year; Valium and wine; increasing fear of a long last illness; more fear of running out of money, being a burden. I sensed her longing to be off, out of here, elsewhere. What was left for her here? More punishment. The prolonged battle with a man who had maimed and abandoned her. Friends—and I had seen and met her new friends, friends tied by cards and proximity only, one of whom said earlier that day, on the phone, "I knew your dear mother for four years, Nicki. She was the kindest, most thoughtful of women—but I didn't know her at all."

I had resented Mama because she had capitulated. Was it her greatest talent, that she could bear so much? She wanted to put down the cross that day and I am now sure that she had borne her grief, deeper than I would ever know, with a private and lonely dread. She had written not a word of it down; I had searched everywhere in the little apartment for some personal statement, some note, some diary. There was nothing personal. It was as if she had wanted to eliminate the personal from her life, that it pained her. She had also kept her fingers off my soul for twenty years, glimpsing, perhaps, that this was the only gift she had for me. I felt I had done nothing for her. I did not know who she was. Had she traveled all that distance, from the muddy farm, from bright dreams and scalding love, to end like this, in such an antiseptic little room, with gray drapes and a gray rug and a gold velour couch, with twenty decks of cards on her shelf? Why hadn't all the words I had learned taught me to say anything to this woman? Did the words have no practical value whatsoever? I thought that they did. That words made the world. In the beginning was the word and the word was all and the word brought light and understanding.

I had one last picture in my brain of my old mama, woozy on who knows what pills and high blood pressure. It was that last time I saw her. She had rambled and repeated and put her hand to her forehead, in dizziness, and then her head in her hands for a moment, and I had said nothing beyond asking, "Are you all right? And she had said she was just fine. She was in our crowded, noisy apartment and then later, on leaving, on the stairway down, she had touched Paul's curly hair—like, I now know, Nat Ress's hair—rubbing it, smiling, as she had often smiled so many years before, without artifice, as if lit by current.

Eight-thirty, nine o'clock. I grew animated, high-strung. I tried to say a few words to my afternoon companion, could not, retreated into my reveries, thumbed through the old family photographs yet again, felt my stomach pinch with hunger, and then sat back and listened as the mute young man finally found his tongue. "It's really better this way, sir," he said. "Quick." He snapped his fingers. "She couldn't have felt a thing. A twinge maybe." I didn't know the trouble some of them have. His own grandmother, who died last year at ninety-two, lived in hell for seven years. First she lost her right leg. Had to be amputated. Diabetes. Bedsores. Shingles. Then the other leg, only from the knee down this time. Then . . . When he had finished with his grandmother the monochromatic monologue went on to other relatives and their sad histories, mingled with cases he had known—colitis, kidney failure, gout, the effects of a stroke if you *didn't* die, half a dozen cancers, lingering disasters I could not have imagined, and their hospital expenses. It was Foxe's *Book of Martyrs*, that unrelenting chronicle of Protestants burned and beheaded at the hands of papist royalty. I kept trying to hold in the great laugh, like a fart in the classroom. It was like a terrible Russian novel. And this clown went on and on, in doleful litany, about more amputations and broken hips, and a dose of Parkinson's shakes—all demonstrated with deadpan face and animated hands, to the accompaniment of the stink of my old mother's remains.

She would not have had the courage for any of this fellow's book of woes. She had been spared that.

I needed a living voice so I called Mari. I told her that we were still waiting for the medical examiner and she said quietly that I should come home soon: "We love you and we need you here. The kids want you here. I want you."

A few moments later the phone rang. It was the funeral chapel. After the interminable wait, more than nine hours now, the medical examiner, pressed with a flood of deaths that wet March Sunday, had signed the papers without seeing the body, ensuring that I would now never know the exact cause of my mother's death beyond its speed, beyond "probable stroke." The chapel was authorized to pick up the papers and come for the remains. They would be there within an hour.

I called Amie and Mari again. Amie said it was "about god-damn time."

Two men soon arrived with papers. When they handed them to my young friend, he pointed to the bathroom. One of the men said, "Let's just get her out of here quick" and the other whispered, "Not in that position." I knew from the crack-ing sounds that they had to bend her, from sitting to lying, and I heard their muffled grunts, the snapping of bone, and then the sound of a zipper. In another moment or two they came out of the alcove with a green bag on a stretcher and I did not think of Saint Theresa in her wild lament but of my old mama in the photograph at the Laurel House, one leg kicking high— and then I rushed home to be with my family.

THERE REMAINED ONLY the funeral and burial. Mama had informed me a year earlier that there was a family plot in Queens. I had told her not to mention such things for another ten years but she said we had to talk about them: that was life. I called several cousins, got the name of the place, and gave it to the funeral parlor.

Amie was in tears when she came to my apartment the day before the funeral. I had not seen her since long before Mama died but had spoken to her more in the past few days than I had in the previous ten years. I put my arm around her as I had never done before and patted her back. She was larger than I remembered but had on just as much garish jewelry. She could barely speak a complete sentence. "That bastard . . . murdered her," she said. "Destroyed her."

"She didn't die of a broken heart," I said.

"She died of grief."

I told Amie what I had done, the arrangements I had made—the funeral chapel, the plot, the people I had called, the wording of the notice I had put in the *Times*. I wanted her to know and approve of everything.

"At least Arthur got his," she said. "He got his, all right."

I knew little about my stepfather. He had called once, to ask me to help with an alimony problem. I simply said it would be inappropriate. He asked nothing about my family but I told him, "You ought to meet them all someday. They're terrific kids—very open, full of energy." He said that his new family wouldn't understand.

Amie told me that he had gotten an immediate vice presidency at the large insurance firm, just like he'd planned. "He got that right after he married his little cutie. But he wanted the number one spot, the bastard. He wanted the prize, all the marbles, what he had been after all of his life. He'd screwed for it and he could taste it."

I asked her what had happened. She was not crying anymore and her eyes were lit with animation.

"He went to the Bahamas. It must have been the vacation

of triumph. It was locked up. Yeah, locked up. At the next board meeting he was going to become the big cheese." I leaned toward my sister. "But it didn't happen that way."

"It didn't?"

"I used to think of him down there: lying in the sun and picturing what it would be like; eating conch at some posh restaurant and barely being able to concentrate on what was being said because he was already in the big president's office, on top of them all, for life. I don't know whether he called his office. I wish I knew. He probably told them to call him if they needed him, if something important came up. Sure. That's what he'd have done. He needed the rest. It isn't easy going after the golden ring all your life and then suddenly being able to kiss it with your fucking lips."

"Well, what happened?" I was growing impatient.

"The bastard got what he deserved, that's what happened," she said. "They kicked him out."

"They did what?"

"His office was locked when he came back. His secretary was gone. There was a letter for him on her desk. He got no notice. That was it. He was out—that day. And he's been a business broker since then. And he's still trying to make his first deal. He takes all of these big-time guys to the golf club, to dinner; he works for weeks, months, trying to get the right people together and then to cough up the big green—months, even years it takes to work out one good deal. You get ten percent, sometimes of three or four million bucks. But he hasn't put one deal together yet." I wondered how Amie knew all this. "He's with his little cutie, but she owns him. She's more than twenty years younger and she owns everything—the car, the golf-club membership, his meals, his balls. He doesn't take a subway without she allows it." She smiled and clicked her lips.

"You forgive Arthur for not paying?" she asked suddenly. Her voice was incredulous. "All her misery these last years— you forgive him that? He could have worked. You do. He could have gotten some sensible middle-level job, where he belonged anyway, because he was mediocre, all the way through, in everything he did. He thought he was important potatoes, but he was ten bucks a dozen—with big dreams."

"There is some poetic justice in—"

"Poetic justice?" my sister roared. "The only justice he deserves is a sharp kick in the groin. And he still owes the alimony, of course."

I told her I'd thought the obligation died with Mama and that if she couldn't get it, and if he was broke, there probably wasn't any chance of collecting. But Amie said that Mama was a pushover and that there was surely money there and that she was going to get it, and that even if there wasn't, it didn't matter.

"What doesn't matter?" I asked.

"Whether he has it. Whether he has any money or not."

"I suppose you can't collect what isn't there."

Amie frowned. "You're as bad as Mama, and I can see you just haven't thought this thing through clearly. I made some calls last night. I called my lawyer and the way I see it is this: the bastard must owe thirty or forty thousand and you have to go to court but my lawyer works on a percentage and he is a demon and is sure to find something." Right after the funeral, she said, I should announce that I was "bound and determined"—she repeated the words—to pursue this thing to the last penny, no matter how long it took; at least it would squeeze him, let him know exactly how we felt. She paused for a moment, then said, "I'd trade anything if I could just kick him in the balls real hard." And she kicked a chair.

Suddenly, unsummoned, images of Arthur came into my head: shoveling and stoking coal together in the dusty basement in Brooklyn, early in the morning or late at night. The two of us at the Polo Grounds the day the Japanese bombed Pearl Harbor—Ace Parker's passes, the announcements, the report from the cabdriver. At Ebbets Field in the heyday of the Dodgers, cheering together as Jackie Robinson charged home from third, on a brilliant steal. Ping-Pong with him at the Mount Vernon home. The two of us trying to make poached eggs one morning when Mama was ill, breaking six into the boiling water, cursing and laughing together. His gigantic pride when I was accepted at the Wharton School . . . and how he said, when I demurred, that I would be "asinine" not to go. Mama had told me, her eyes wet, that he once claimed to have married her for me; and I had even chosen the man for a father.

But if chalk was chalk, Arthur was a bastard. He crunched lives mechanically, full of self-righteousness. Once he had talked of going up to Harlem with a batch of guys and baseball bats. (I was eleven or so and thought it was to play a baseball game.) Still, if he had no money, was chasing him worth the effort? And could he have tried all those years and simply failed? Could he have made one mistake, thirty-eight years earlier, marrying Mama for all the wrong reasons, but then suffered because *she* had been hell to live with? He had been an outsider from the beginning in Mama's family. None of the large clan accepted him. Grandma used to say, "You know, this one is not like the other one. I don't like this one." Open and ebullient, the Bernsteins had all hated his cool, literal ways, his low jokes, his cards tight to his vest. They had not accepted him and neither had I. I had given him obedience, lies, hypocrisy. What would Mama gain now from a protracted legal action against this man?

"What are you thinking of, Nicki? Where are you? Do you know that you are *bound by law* to pursue this matter?" She leaned across the table. "As the executor of the estate, you are legally compelled to collect all money owed her if I say so. Promptly. Do you understand that, Nicki?"

"Yes," I said quietly.

Would it do any good now? Any good whatsoever? Mama was dead. Was it moral to hound the man to *his* grave? Was it moral *not* to pursue the matter? Should I pursue this thing, perhaps, precisely because Arthur would be counting his blessings right now that Mama had died, would be counting on me dropping the matter, just as he had in his calculating way counted on so much acquiescence from the three of us over the years? And was it perhaps important for me, even now, to do this thing, to stand against the man as, clearly, I had not stood against him or almost anyone, perhaps because of him, in my life? I survived not by standing against people but by holding my head under water longer than they could.

"You are *determined* to press this thing, with all necessary force and resolve, Nicki? No matter how painful it may become?"

I did not answer. I was thinking of all the pictures I had looked at that long day in her apartment, the odor that said all was scurrying toward this decay.

"I'd like to hear your words on this. I want to know whether you'll undertake this campaign. He had a heart attack, a little one, about two years ago; it may be a painful action. Will you stand by it? For both the principle and the money that he owes us?"

I looked closely at Amie. Her face was now taut and tense. Her eyes were narrow. She wanted this connection—to Arthur, to me. I had always wanted to be separate, apart.

"Yes, Amie," I said, extending my hand and grasping her forearm firmly, knowing that I would not want to share in any proceeds that came from this source but that I would pursue them—for her, for Mama. I did not precisely know why but understood that somehow it was what I had to do. It would take time away from my work and my emotional energy which I guarded zealously. "Yes," I said, "I am determined to press this thing, with force and resolve, no matter how painful it is to anyone."

THOUGH AMIE INSISTED upon having the casket closed, when I got to the chapel an hour early, to make sure all the arrangements were in order, the box was open. Mama looked peaceful to me, beneath a dull red light. They had not put too much makeup on, as I had expected. I knew her. I knew this shell. You could even see, behind the face, faint traces of the young woman who had been in the photographs, in the photograph with Nat Ress centuries earlier. You could if you looked closely, if you had some imagination.

I sat by the casket for about ten minutes, unable to take my eyes from her face.

"Shall I close it now, sir?" an attendant asked. He was a pleasant man, not all sepulchral as I had supposed.

"I guess so," I said. I did not want Amie to come in with it open.

He unfastened one of the props that kept it open.

"Another minute or two," I said, and when he stepped back I unwrapped a single lily that I had bought on the walk from our apartment to the chapel. It was small and white and quite delicate. I placed it gently on her breast, looked at the relaxed face again, and raised my hand to indicate that the attendant should continue.

The service was brief.

I put on a yarmulke for the first time in many years; the rabbi pinned a black ribbon to my lapel and then pinned one to Amie. Then he bade us repeat a few simple words in Hebrew; they sounded foreign, strange to my ears. When we came to the end, the attendant cut a tear in the black cloth above my heart with a swift stroke.

Perhaps fifteen people had come—her new women friends, two of her younger cousins, several people I didn't recognize, Mari, and two of our children. My children looked very handsome and curious; this was their first death and they were closer to my mother than I had been. Jenny cried; my son, Charlie, did not. At the door, a dowdy old woman came up to me and said: "Are you the son?" I nodded. "It's the first day of spring and God has taken another flower to heaven." I doubted she had known Mama. The day was blustery and cold and wet.

Amie, Mari, and the two children drove with me in the black limousine to the cemetery, a long car behind the somber hearse. We were the only mourners. Mama's casket was placed on a rack over the hole and the rabbi said a few words, in Hebrew and then in English, and within moments motioned for us to return to the car, out of the rain.

"Is that all?" asked Amie, not moving. She had been silent all the way out. She had wept when she'd first entered the chapel.

"That's all," I whispered. "He didn't know Mama. What else could he say?"

"Don't we throw dirt on it, or something?"

"No," the rabbi said. "It's not called for."

"Well, it's too brief."

The rabbi again motioned us to leave—he seemed in a hurry—but I stood still a moment longer with most of my little family, holding Amie's hand. I noticed that I was holding some roses and gave one to each of them and tossed mine into the grave and gestured that the others could drop their roses down after Rose, who had not had such a good time of it here.

Then I looked across the gray sea of stones, the silent acres and acres of minor monuments, and then at the stones near the raw hole beside which we stood. A couple of diggers leaned on their shovels, a discreet distance to the left. The rain had turned all of the exposed soil to mud. I turned my head slightly, to the stone just to the left of where my mother's stone would go, and there, with some dates, the last one in March 1932, three months before I was born, was my name, "Nathan Ress."

It was just an old stone, with some dates and a name. It wasn't much and I'm not sure why, but I felt a heavy shock of disbelief and recognition and felt that the drama was done.

10

THE LAST GAME

Sometime in my late forties, I glanced at myself in a mirror and saw that I had been transformed over the years into a hippopotamus. I made a few furtive walks to the Riverside Park basketball courts and in time it came to me that I might have a few games left in me. With faint hopes and dreams, I thought of that time when I weighed 150 and lived for the hoop.

I had bloomed late. Though I had not played any high school ball, I fought my way onto the freshman team at Penn, past recruited ballplayers and men who had made all-state in high school. And then I spent three long years on the varsity as a sub-sub, my chief pleasure watching Ernie Beck, my friend and classmate, make All-America and lead us to the Ivy League championship in 1953. Dick Harter, who later became such a superb coach, was on that team, too, always talking basketball—and I remember Dick Dougherty's wise body-wit and Don Scanlon's jumper, some extraordinary left-hand drives by Bobby "Kangaroo" Brooks, Tim Holt's lithe speed, and the day Howie Dallmar arranged a scrimmage with the Minneapolis Lakers and Slater Martin scooted around Vern Mikkelsen and Jim Pollard and George Mikan and made me feel as though I had two broken legs and blurred vision.

Ernie used to pray and cross himself in the locker room before each game—and then get twenty-five points. I began to pray for Howie Dallmar to put me in. It didn't work. Once, when our game aired on television, I dribbled downcourt by myself, in those familiar last two minutes when all the subs go in and chaos reigns, and threw the basketball neatly over the backboard. I finally won a full letter in my senior year, and the Bill Wollman Award for the Best Junior Varsity Player (though there wasn't a JV then); my name is still on a plaque in the Palestra. But in my entire dubious career I scored only three points. All on foul shots. All at Dartmouth, during Winter Carnival. I had given the game every ounce of will and passion I could muster at five foot nine, with no high school experience behind me, but I had not gone nearly so far as my colossal dreams dictated.

In the Army, in my early twenties, I suddenly came into my own, a couple of years too late. If only Howie could have seen me burn up the league in western France that year! At 148 pounds, just out of basic training, I could touch the rim, average twenty-two points a game, and lead a no-bench team from the dingy little post at Croix-Chapeau to a divisional championship at Bordeaux and into the All-France playoffs in Paris.

That had been a double elimination tournament and we had
played SHAPE first, a team of ringers collected by some ego-
maniac sports colonel. They had two guys who later made All-
America (one of them six foot six), an ex-Globetrotter, and a
five-foot-eight kid who jumped center and could dunk. We had
no one taller than six-one.

In the middle of our pregame warm-up, we stopped our
own shooting and merely watched, wide-eyed.

But we pressed full-court, the five of us, and hustled like
mad the entire game, and somehow we beat them by a point in
double overtime. I scored thirty-five points. It was the high
moment of my little career. My eighty-yard run. And I wished
with my heart that Dallmar had seen it.

After an interminable night of visiting half a dozen bars in
Paris, we comfortably lost to SHAPE two days later by a mere
53 points.

When my three boys were small I used to tell them about
those good old Army days. On a long noisy trip home from the
country, I would tell the one about our winning the regional
championship by taking two out of three games in two days. At
first they were awed and quiet. Later, when my weight rose to
195, then soared blithely over 200, Paul and Charles would
interrupt.

"We *know* how you once won those games in two days,
Dad—"

"And how the games were played in a field hangar—"

"—that was so dark you couldn't see the ball under the
baskets—"

"—and so cold they had heat blowers at half-court."

I would say: "They really did. Big, red heaters. At
mid-court."

"And how you scored seventy-six points—"

"Seventy-eight."

"—in the three games, all played within twenty-four hours. One the first night, two the next morning and afternoon. And how the opposing fans would trip you if you got too close to their sidelines, and spit on the cement floor of the hangar, and the refs never saw any of it."

"Did it *really* happen?" asked Anthony, my youngest, his eyes wide; he had heard the story only four or five times before. "Just like that?"

"Just like that," I mumbled. "Many, many pounds ago."

But as the years went on, I wondered. There were no witnesses I could summon to vouch for my brief hour of glory. All that remained of all those desperate, passionate years of training and hoping was the faded scroll that announced I had been awarded a varsity letter in 1953.

My most vivid memories were of half-court ball at Wingate Field. It had been a whole world, the only world to me in Brooklyn, before I went to Penn, with its regular cast of characters and its own patois.

In our park, during my high-school years, we had Natey, George, Herbie, Stanley, the Commissioner (I never knew him by any other name), Hooks (nor him), Artie, Ira, Mike, and the Marine (who looked it, always wore fatigues, and rarely spoke). We played in the dead of winter, carrying our own shovels to the park and clearing enough space to play—the cold so sharp our lungs heaved until we coughed and gagged, our frozen fingers too stiff to manage a ball. We had a joke about those guys like George who had one unbelievable push shot, banked from the right side: that he practiced all winter with gloves and came down at night and shot for hours by the faint light from the park lamp. He was lethal from his one spot. And from nowhere else.

The pole was attached directly beneath the backboard, and you could not take a truly hard-driving layup without either crashing into it or grasping it as soon as the ball left your hands, and then swinging around it like a monkey. People new to the court rarely left unscarred after an afternoon of ball with us, both from their own untutored moves and because we ceremoniously used the pole as a pick. I had only two serious confrontations with the pole: once, on a desperately determined drive, my knee went into it and turned to jelly for a month (I made the shot); and once my forehead met it squarely, opened like a can, and took seven stitches that afternoon.

Whenever I could, I returned to the park and managed to get in four or five good games before dark.

"Nobody quits," we would say on a dreamy June afternoon after twenty or thirty hard games, which had begun about eight in the morning and been interrupted only for a popsicle or two from Sam's pushcart for lunch. "Nobody like us, like the *real guys*, ever stops playing basketball. Nobody ever kicks the habit."

"Yeah. Who'd want to?" asked George.

"I'll play till I'm eighty," I said.

But even before I went into the Army, there were defections. Several of the older boys went into business and of course were not seen at all during the week. On weekends in November when the trees were sere and the games hottest, they were pale portly remnants of our older heroes, snuggled into loose topcoats from which protruded dress slacks and dress shoes. One of them even began to smoke a cigar. I remember watching them that fall—three, four of the regulars—sitting on the bench outside the fence, caged away from all that was life, talking, kibitzing about a move or shot, remembering perhaps, never playing.

Did it finally come to that?

I felt closer to a guy named Schnaiter or Schlotter who was twenty-six and had tried out for the Knicks for five years running, though he'd never played college ball. He was a ball bum, an addict, and he's probably at Wingate to this day, hooping merrily. I was at Penn then, last man, but that did not keep me from vaguely wondering now and then whether I too should not try out for the Knicks someday. I was still improving and Wat Misaka had played and was gone.

But later, during my last months in the Army, I began to read with far more intensity than ever I had brought even to half-court. Still later, when I went back to school, suddenly, somehow, mysteriously, basketball was gone. Poof. I was years behind and there was time for nothing but reading—more Joyce, Proust now, Morris Croll on "The Baroque Style in Prose," nasty delicious Waugh, Pushkin and Goncharov and Babel—dazzling, athletic minds—and then marrying, fathering, and all those jobs, jobs that tore into the passion I had fanned with such a fine and fresh fury.

And suddenly I was pushing fifty and over two hundred pounds.

Poof.

My three boys had all taken a liking to the game, and for several years I had gone to the Riverside courts to watch them, and even, in my mid-thirties, I'd attempted to make a brief comeback, halted when I fell on my right elbow, which promptly popped a lump the size and color of a plum. Strange. My body did weird things now. All my old finger fractures started to swell up, my ankles were as stiff as candy canes, there was no rubber left in my arches, and I would get sharp, deep pains in my chest.

But there seemed a little left, a few good moves. And how I still loved the game—the rhythm and force of it, the blurring, twisting sensuousness of it, the speed and quickness of a drive, fake, spin, and shot.

I wondered if Ernie was still playing, how much *he* had left. I had last seen him twenty-five years earlier after a preseason Philadelphia Warriors game in Poughkeepsie: in the locker room, having his ankles untaped, he told me of the tours he had taken that summer, how many games he had played. He smiled when I told him, for some reason, that I was currently passionate about a guy name Rilke. Beck looked weary to the bone.

The names had changed but many of the same types were at the Riverside courts: a bell-shaped waddler with a lethal one-hand push—or heave; a guy who habitually played in dark glasses, a blue shirt with a little alligator on the breast, and pointed suede shoes—and had an incredibly long, seemingly off-balance two-handed shot that only occasionally missed: we'd had one like him, too. Half a dozen players had those curiously defined stances and shots that characterize the pathological half-court player: a ball shift in midair and then a left-handed shot (and practically no other discernible talent); a magnet *only* from the left corner.

The one full-court game was dominated by big, lean, highly competitive men, eighteen to thirty, who played regularly and with all the flair and speed that have come to characterize the best of the city game. They were strong, agile high leapers, and often hardmouthed. "It's a tough game, little man," one said to me the day I tripped and went over on my elbow. God, I'd have loved to be nineteen or twenty again and run with them all day.

But I did not especially want to play Dick Diver in front of my oldest sons, who were getting sharper on the courts every day.

Several times I went down early on a Saturday or Sunday, to practice alone. The game, like fishing, helped me soften the tensions of my life. When I played, I was sure to choose a court with fourteen-year-olds or old-timers, and to use my head more than my body. The hardest part was remembering what I once could have done—and seeing how paltry was the music I could wring from my aging instrument. Now and then someone would jock me—make two or three effective, scoring moves, block one or two of my shots—and I would feel that fierce competitive drive burn like acid in my brain and I would want to let out the wolf, take on the guy with all my force, chew him up.

I held back. Always I tried to smile and let my man have his day. I had had mine. Briefly. Long ago. In another country.

Then, on a gorgeous day in mid-April, a day all at once cool and calm and bright, I decided to check myself out, good and proper, on the courts. Alone. At midday. Perhaps there was something left.

No one would be there, and I could see exactly how much was left of the famous Lyons double-pump, the jumper, the quick moves I had always depended upon. My fingers were stiff but usable; my chest still hurt, but only when I breathed hard. Green buds were fuzzy on the park trees, and limberly I skipped and scuffed my feet a few times on the way down to the park, whistling, like in the old days.

The four courts were deserted.

I left my bush coat on and began close to the hoop—layups without dribbling, short turnaround jumpers, a left-handed hook, a few wrong-side twists from underneath. I remembered Septembers at Penn and the same ritual and the huge hopes I would always have for each new year.

A few shots went in but there was a heaviness in my arms, a stiffness in my fingers. I moved out a few feet and tried a few more jumpers. Short. Too hard. A little to the side. There wasn't much of a touch left. Maybe they had raised the rim. I seemed farther from it on my layups, farther than I'd been that year in the Army—four, five inches from the rim now.

I took off my bush coat and flexed my shoulders back hard several times. I jumped up and down for five minutes on the balls of my feet, to loosen my arches. I tried a longer jumper and nearly tripped over my feet. I tried a few old moves—faking once, twice, then sweeping right, toward the basket.

Maybe there was a *little* left to work with.

Maybe.

I felt a bit of power in the turn, authority, some of the old quickness. Double-pump then up, underhand, softly. *Yes.* Dribble out to the foul line, fake, jump, the ball held high, higher . . . yes. Another jumper. *Swish.* And another two. *Swish. Swish.*

The body remembered something.

Fifteen minutes of that—making more and more shots, having the sweet satisfaction of watching a decent percentage go in now, feeling the hard-earned grace recalled in arm and leg—and I knew it was still possible to enjoy this thing that had been my youth. I began to look for a couple of guys to play with. *A little hoop, a little b-ball.* My children would not be out of school for another two hours. There was now a two-man game in progress on the end court but it did not look like much. Another hour of practice would be best.

A lean twenty-year-old with a mustache came over and began to shoot with me. He had a fair jump shot. Then two more young men came over—one five-ten, about 180 pounds, built like a soccer player; he kicked the ball a few times, bounced it off his head, and I knew he was. The other was high on something. We shot for sides and I got to play with the guy who was high, and to cover the soccer player.

Something is going to go, I thought suddenly. *The fingers probably.*

The soccer player was all over me, fouling me, waving his arms madly, having a splendid time pounding the hell out of me. I did not call foul. In the old days I rarely did. It slowed down the game.

I played tentatively, trying a fake, seeing what my man would do, letting my insanely wild teammate shoot the first five shots. They were all slammed against the backboard; only one even touched the rim. Our slim opponent dropped five one-handers in a row; he was a ballplayer.

I made a short jumper, then a left-handed layup, then a delayed pump. I got a few rebounds and felt my body grow hungry for harder play. I elbowed the soccer player away twice, slipped behind him and stole the ball, played weasel-quick. Not much of a game, not very good ballplayers—but I was enjoying myself. You have to learn to work within your limits, that's all. It was not even a game in which I would have played in the old days, but I was moving deftly now. I could score at will against the strong and awkward soccer player, without pressing too hard, without embarrassing him. No need to do that. I set up my teammate twice: he made one of the shots, from underneath, all alone, on a pick-and-roll worthy of the name. He had not seen where the ball came to him from. Even my passing was getting sharp.

The lean opponent dropped two more jumpers, the soccer player sent one flying from halfcourt two-handed, and it swished. He tried to ram into me on a drive but I sidestepped sharply, dipped behind him with my right hand, and, without touching him, stole the ball. Twice I outpositioned him under the boards and, though he jumped on my back, I scooted away with the rebound.

There was not *something* but a lot left. The chest pains were not too severe, my ankles were holding. I was slipping into the rhythm of the thing.

Swish. Two more: one jumper, one drive from the left. The soccer player whammed me but I made the shot anyway. And we won.

I sat down on the green bench outside the fence, pleased with myself—sweating profusely but damned pleased. I was in the game again. I could still do this thing. I would drop a bit more weight this month and then I'd be able to regain even more of what I'd once had.

The courts began to fill up now. The regulars were arriving for the full-court game. I watched them: a couple of six-foot-four black guys; a blond seventeen-year-old I had been following all spring; a guy with a wild Afro, about five-eight, who dunked; Mel, a slim young black who put the bite on me for fifty cents again; Dick, a football player, in from college. They jostled one another under the boards for a free ball, took long one-handers.

Not for me. Not anymore. They were too young, too strong,

too quick, too aggressive. Enough. I had had one good game.
My boys would be down in an hour; I could watch them. I
could be that much of a fan. And I could remember.

"Holly—woooood!" Mel said, making one of his strange
one-handers as if guided by the divine afflatus. "All right, you
mothers. A little ball. Les' play a game. I din' come here to
shoot. Les' play."

I got up from the bench to retrieve my ball. It was not the
best there and they would not need it. As I came around the
fence, another ball bounced toward me and I took it, dribbled
once, and shot. *Swish.* "Holly—woooood!" shouted Mel, nodding his approval to me. "All right, these two here beeg mens
choose 'em up and we play a little bas-ket-ball."

I walked toward the gate. They were choosing up sides and
Mel had taken charge. I turned to listen to his quick patter and
heard him coach one of the captains: "Take that there little
white feller. One with the curly hair. There. He's sma-*art.*
Smart ballplayer. Per-fessor. I'm a per-fessor, too. I per-fess. I
con-fess. I de-press and jus press."

The man motioned me onto his team.

Well, if Mel really thought I was worth picking, I ought to
give it a try. I hadn't played so badly before. I could run with
them, full-court, for a half hour. With Mel on my team we
would at least be in the game.

Two minutes into the ballgame they gave the ball to the
smart player. He was all alone on the right side, took a quick
step after bobbling the ball, and jumped for a shot. Someone,
he never knew who, swatted it cleanly into the fence before it
had gone an inch. Two plays later they gave it to him again. He
was, by now, panting wildly. All the old will to win was back in
him. He drove for the basket, bobbled the ball again, took six

or seven steps, felt like a perfect asshole, and was properly called for walking. He noticed that he who had called the walk was Mel, who was therefore not on his side but the other.

Euchred.

I was the dud. The lemon. I knew it now and so did everyone else on my team. And the other team. They huddled and my man, the lanky seventeen-year-old, left me completely on defense and double-teamed my team's ace, a lefty with springs for arches. On offense, the kid took me right into the pivot twice and scored twice, quite quickly.

Someone muttered, "Turkey."

But I played with the great Beck. I'm the only guy here who played college ball. In my day I could run rings around all of you, I thought, getting my second wind, then my third, working my way into position, calling for the ball, hustling back on defense, stealing the ball on their fast break with a move I had learned from Timmy Holt, then losing the ball, moving always without the ball (since they appeared determined, now, not to let me touch it).

Two jumpers and I can salvage this disaster. A good double-pump, like the old days, and they'll know who I am. Like that time in the hangar, when the French shouted, Comme ça, *un danseur.* And that's what I had been: graceful, lithe, a fantastic leaper. Once. *Hang in. A little longer.*

I glanced toward the sidelines, now packed with onlookers. My children weren't there. Neither were any of their hoop friends, who would have told. Neither was Dallmar.

I heard the word "turkey" again, and blanched. Ten to eight, theirs. We could still pull this one out, and in the second game I could come into my own. I knew I had enough left. I knew I could still play in this league. I had played with Beck!

"Holly—woooood!" shouted Mel, making his fifth straight shot from nearly half-court, dancing, clowning afterward.

I felt a twinge in my left leg. Nothing to worry about there. I had never had problems with my calves. When I went, it would be an ankle, or the chest (which hurt not at all now), or the elbow again, or the fingers.

Up and back. Up and back down again. Our left-handed ace was keeping us in the game with his long jumpers. The score was sixteen apiece. We could still win.

We?

My opponents' opponents were playing with four men. They didn't see me anymore. I was racing back and forth, diving for the ball, calling for the ball, playing a sort of butcher-shop defense, now and then taking the ball out, but never being given the ball when there was a threat that I would do something like shoot or dribble, never past half-court.

Then it happened.

Quickly. With finality.

I leaped with all my might for a rebound, fully ten feet away from the ball, and felt the muscles tear and the sharp, splintery pain in my left calf.

I put my foot down ever so gently and collapsed. I could not support myself. The pain was so excruciating that I could hardly hobble to our nearest man and beg him, in a cracked voice, to get a replacement. He had been a poker-faced, hard-nosed, unsmiling player the entire game. He wanted nothing more than to win, as I had once—with all my heart—wanted to win whenever I played. He looked slowly down at my leg, supported gingerly by my big toe, and a broad smile spread rapidly across his face. Replacement? Sure. Sure. He'd get a replacement. It would be a pleasure.

I was done. Probably for months. Perhaps, at last, forever.

It took me nearly an hour to walk the eight blocks home. I clutched the basketball in my left hand, against my body, and flexed the perfectly limber fingers of my right. I saw nothing but the pavement in front of me. Each step was hell. Every curb was an Everest.

At least my boys had not been there. Perhaps I would take them to Philadelphia someday and show them my name in the Palestra. That sounded like the safe kind of thing a retired old hooper, looking for a moment of the past regained, ought to do.

The courts were surely no country for this old man.

11

AMIE

Five months after I buried my mother in that gray field next to a father I'd never known, my half sister, Amie died. She was thirty-six. It happened like this: I had returned the night before from a trip to England, during which I'd agreed to develop a book publishing subsidiary for an old British firm. I called Amie about nine-thirty in the morning. With the little money we had inherited from Mama, she had decided to start a nail salon, on the second floor of a low building overlooking East Twenty-third Street. A couple of my children had printed and distributed flyers for her, I'd seen her shop and met Alphonse, a carpenter she thought she might marry, and in the two weeks

I was in London, I knew it must have opened. I was anxious to speak with her.

We had not precisely grown close, but we had seen or spoken to each other several times a week since Mama died—sometimes on estate matters, sometimes just to talk. In an odd way, Mama's death had cut her free, injected her with a certain shot of new life. She was happier than I could remember ever having seen her. She was suddenly interested in everything I could tell her about my children, their schoolwork, their friends; she found their escapades hilarious. In the prior ten years she had never asked a question about them. I enjoyed the development of some relationship after so many years and she was eager for the connection. Once, when we were walking with Mari, I felt her tug at my arm, wanting to have me closer. Mari could not warm to her but Tony and Jenny did, and all of my children enjoyed any relative, were happy to have found one, with her blue-black coiffed hair with a pearl in its center. I had kept up connections with none of my relatives. She brought all four of my children presents and gabbed with them on the phone and remained adamant about my pressing the alimony suit against Arthur Lyons. "That bastard has to pay every nickel," she insisted. "Remember that, Nicki. I won't let you settle for a nickel less than he owes."

When we had cleaned Mama's apartment, I had given her full authority to make all decisions regarding real property, little that there was. Mama's will, which was invalid on a technicality, had given Amie all of the property; though in effect Mama had died intestate, I did not hesitate to honor what she'd wanted. Amie went through the little L-shaped apartment like a tornado, bashing everything before her. "Junk, junk, junk," she said, tossing out arms full of dresses, slacks, drawers full of papers wholesale. Now and then, increasingly nervous, I'd see her plunge something into a great green garbage bag and I'd thrust my hand in after it and she'd say, "It's all mine, isn't it?" and if it was something I wanted badly, I'd say, "Well this is just something I might like to have, if you really don't want it," and after I'd said that four or five times a strange sort of resignation went through me: I didn't want to fight with my half-sister; I didn't want her to have one more authority in her life. I wanted to keep everything, even scraps of paper, some connection to a world I had neglected and denied, fragments I might someday put into a coherent whole, and yet with deep breaths I looked away and I have to this day, forty years later, no sure sense of what parts of my life, what secrets, went into the green bags.

We started to clean the apartment no more than ten minutes after the state appraiser left. An hour into the work, there was a phone call from a dealer, obviously tipped off, saying he paid cash for jewelry, silver, anything of value. Amie's face lit up and widened when the buyer came with a fat wad of bills, showed no interest in Mama's old mink or the china, and, before I could protest, she sold the family silver—flatware, serving spoons and forks, sugar bowls, a large plate, salt and pepper shakers. The dealer had been told exactly where it was. I told Amie I would buy the silver decanter, with six small wine vessels, engraved by his temple for my grandfather, and she pulled those away from the dealer at the last moment. In the end, the residue of my mother's lifetime, everything except the photographs and a handful of randomly saved papers, went into green bags or the hands of that dealer. When we left, well into the evening, there were thirty-odd green bags scattered in that small room, like some bizarre postmodern sculpture.

I initiated an action against Arthur but the lawyer saw little chance of collecting any portion of the unpaid alimony. Amie badgered me about it regularly, and Arthur's sister—whom I had always liked—called me twice to ask that I desist.

MARI, JENNIFER, AND Tony had been with me in England but I had returned two days early, to prepare for my classes. We had been away for two weeks.

"Hi!" Amie said with animation when I called her that Monday morning about nine-thirty. "I have a thousand things to tell you." She began to chatter away about the nail salon, and about Alphonse . . . then suddenly said, "Oh, I feel dizzy," and her voice fractured and gave way to anguished guttural sounds. The sounds were terrible, the ugliest of gargling noises, and then there was the sound of something falling to the ground, and sharp barking from her two Yorkies. Then silence.

I called her name four or five times—first as a question, then louder, as if I thought loudness might better be heard. Was something wrong with the phone? Had wires in the receiver gone awry? I could still hear the dogs barking, but fainter, as if they were farther away or some cloth was covering the phone.

What to do?

I knew no one in her building. I didn't think to call the police. I hung up the phone and rapidly dialed again. There was a busy signal. Was she talking to someone?

A few minutes later I rushed out of my apartment in the West Eighties and took a cab to her apartment in the East

Thirties. What could have happened? That gargling sound had been terrible, never to be forgotten.

The super was in the basement and after having banged on Amie's door over and over, I demanded the key to her apartment. The Yorkies had barked but there'd been was no other sound. The super, an older European woman, shook her head and I shouted that I'd call the police if she didn't give it to me.

Amie was there, flat out on the floor, clutching the phone, the Yorkies, behind the expandable barricade in the kitchen, quiet now, making low sounds, Amie dead still, her crotch stained wet.

For years my dentist, a wit, quipped—when my mouth was propped open and I could not respond—that I should use the telephone sparingly. "Only call people you hate, Nick."

AMIE HAD NO will so my lawyer called Arthur and said that his daughter had died suddenly and that the little estate was his. Arthur asked how much it amounted to, quickly calculated that he'd have to clean the apartment, deal with several lawyers, pay taxes, close all accounts, and in the end there would be nothing; so he said he did not want it. For my part, after what Amie had told me I did not want Arthur to have a shoelace of hers and wanted the matter of my mother's uncollectible alimony done with; there was now no one alive who was entitled to it.

His lawyer and mine talked and agreed that Arthur and I should meet in his lawyer's office, just the two of us, without counsel, and sign two documents, one in which Arthur relinquished all interest in Amie's estate in my favor and the other in which I, as executor and now sole heir of my mother's estate, terminated all claims for back alimony.

I HAD NOT seen Arthur in more than fifteen years and the only picture I had of him was that photograph with his ghost image reflected in the glass panel at my wedding. He was seated at a long polished table in his lawyer's conference room, and he raised himself to a half-standing position when he saw me. The table was big enough for several dozen conferees, the room was lined with law volumes, and the broad windows overlooked, to the south, the skyscrapers in the business district and the bay where the Hudson and East Rivers joined. He had aged. He still looked a little like Ray Bolger, the straw man in *The Wizard of Oz*, but he was now twenty pounds heavier than I remembered him—pudgy-faced, lumpy. He had thin gray hair and a slight twist to his mouth that suggested he had had a stroke. He did not quite smile but he tried to smile and when I did not respond he quit it and just said, in a low, husky voice, "Hi, Nicki."

I did not remember that voice. I remembered the effect of the man on me for those years when he was my stepfather. Words he'd uttered, and when. A certain cold, acid tone. He was not a large man and he was no Prussian officer. But I'd felt his boot and felt his voice slice through me when he'd said it was insane not to accept my acceptance into the Wharton School, "the best business program in the country, damn it." He was tame and gray at the table and I almost pitied him. I said nothing but smiled thinly without opening my lips, and promptly picked up one of the two documents already on the table. They were simple work and we agreed to everything in no more than three minutes. I nodded, took my copy of each document, remembered that the lawyers wanted to see them once again after they had been executed, and put my arms on the arms of the chair, to stand up. But when my stepfather asked me, in that same husky voice, "What happened?" I lowered myself back into the chair, grimaced, and told him that she had died of something while talking to me on the telephone.

"While you were talking to her on the telephone?" He had not heard.

I nodded.

"Heart attack, I suppose," he said. "But she wasn't forty, was she?"

I told him that she was thirty-six and that I hadn't heard from the medical examiner. As with my mother, I never found out, even after I wrote a blistering letter to the examiner's office telling them I wrote for the *New York Times*, threatening to expose them all as incompetents. I found a cabinet full of prescription drugs, marijuana in one of her drawers, a disk of birth control pills on her kitchen table, and I've since heard various theories about some of the possible combinations, most of them leaning toward clots that formed and went to her brain.

When he began to ask questions about her life—what work she was doing, how she lived—I could not forget how she had told me she often drove to his house in Westchester and sat in the dark car, waiting for a glimpse of him, how she'd called him a few times, years earlier, how, the last time she spoke to him, in her mid-twenties, he had said in a barking voice, "Never call me at this number again," and she never had, had in fact never called him on any number again. I was not at first inclined to give the man much information about the life of his only natural child. But he was determined now to know just a bit more and I did not think the details should be denied him. She was starting a nail salon, I told him, because she couldn't get work in the garment district, designing men's shirts, anymore. He knew that she had not remarried and asked me if she was seeing someone.

I said that she was.

"A decent-type person?"

I told my stepfather that I had met the man once and that they liked each other. "Just possibly he had proposed," I said, "and that's what she was going to tell me when . . ."

"What was he . . . what did he do?"

I told him that I'd only met the man briefly, at the nail salon. He'd done the construction. "He was a carpenter, I think. I liked him."

"A car-pen-ter?"

"Alphonse was a carpenter. Yes."

"Alphonse?" he said quietly. "He was French, I suppose."

"Jamaican, I think."

Arthur paused. He looked at me and then looked away. He had always been a good poker player with his emotions and at first I had no idea what he was digging for. And I didn't care. I'd told him too much already. I didn't want to discuss anything with the man. He was just an old man I'd known once. I was ready to leave. We'd completed our business.

"Was he a . . .?" my stepfather asked.

My face flushed hot. "Jamaican," I said slowly, looking him directly in the face.

"Was he a nigger?"

That brutal word. I looked away.

My stepfather was quiet for a moment, then said, tightening his lips, "Maybe it's better she's dead."

Maybe you'd be better dead, you bastard, I thought to say, but simply stood up, half smiled, said I doubted that she was better now than anything, said I thought the lawyers could handle the details, and left, that word, that view of Amie's fortuitous death, final confirmation of all I hated in the man. In a way, hearing him say those words had been satisfying.

I never saw or spoke to him again. When, three years later, he died of a heart attack, I did not for a moment think of going to his funeral. His sister, Florence, with whom I had remained friendly, was insulted that I didn't go, so I told her why, as briefly as I could, and told her that with both my mother and my sister dead I was left to do all the hating, that he hadn't been much to me for a long time; I told her what he had said about Amie. Arthur's best friend, his lawyer, said it was better I had not gone to the funeral. His wife and kids were fine people and it would have been awkward for them. Anyway, he'd never told his four adopted children about me or Amie.

To the end, my stepfather had been lousy with secrets.

SOME MONTHS AFTER Amie died, after the court papers had been approved, the time came to clean her apartment, as I had cleaned Mama's little apartment. Amie had lived in a one-bedroom apartment with four walk-in closets. I had never seen so many clothes outside of Bloomingdale's, where most of the stuff had come from: row after row of tightly packed and very expensive shirts, blouses, suits, sweaters, and coats. Three rows in each closet. There must have been several hundred pieces, many without the price tags removed. There were Gucci, Saint Laurent, Jaeger blouses—ten of each design, in five or six different fabrics and colors. There were more than one hundred pairs of designer shoes, half of them still in their boxes, unworn. I counted thirty-seven handbags from tiny to huge—all Louis Vuitton; fifty or more unopened bottles of perfume; fifteen wristwatches; six radios; three dildos; fifty turtleneck shirts in half a dozen different styles.

Had Amie been a petty thief—or, abandoned by Arthur, always quarreling with Mama, rarely noticed by her older brother, was she just starved for love, giving it to herself on fantastic buying binges, her own best charity?

There was half a pound of marijuana in a drawer of the night table next to her bed. In a valise under her bed I found a note dated a year after her marriage, telling her husband how good the night had been, pleading that they were making progress. Her husband, a trim man who kept his face waxed and wore tight pants, had left her not more than a year after they married, moved to Florida, and was living with a man. In every handbag, in every little box scattered around the apartment, on every open dish, there was a penny—for luck? I found a cache of old photographs: of her at ten, with me, looking up at me on a weekend I was home from college; her wedding pictures, neatly protected in a sheath of velvet cloths; more than one hundred photographs of a succession of Yorkshire terriers, the last two of which I had given to her best friend the afternoon I found her dead. She must have been taking twenty-five different prescription drugs and I merely emptied all the containers and took them home, thinking that someday I would ask a doctor if some combination of them might cause the kind of sudden death she suffered. But I never did, and in one of my spring purges, I chucked them into one of the green garbage bags. There were a couple of dozen books, perhaps two years' selections from the Literary Guild and two Reader's Digest compendiums of condensed books.

There was no skeleton on the bed, like the one in Faulkner's story, but there were the remains in the apartment of a life so alien to mine that I froze and felt the profoundest sadness as I touched each item in the rooms, weighed and considered its future. The pennies everywhere had brought her not a shred of luck. But she wasn't better off dead.

There had been a Blackglama coat worth five or six thousand dollars, which she had bought in her good years, when the fashion world looked like it might provide a great career for her. She loved it, like Mama had loved her moth-eaten mink. Her friends, a hard crew, mostly single, at first said the coat was with Sol Cohen, a furrier. But I could find no receipt for it in her purse or among her papers. She'd had a purse snatched in July—perhaps the claim check was in that. I visited Cohen and he merely said that he knew Amie and had gone to her funeral; in the matter of the Blackglama coat he said: "If you had a receipt, I guess I'd have to give you a coat. But you'd have to have a receipt for that, wouldn't you?" The insurance company said that without a receipt they could bring no case against the furrier Cohen. When I asked Amie's friends again about the coat, all four of them advised me expressionlessly that they knew nothing about such a coat. All had their minks in Cohen's vaults.

That Sunday I held an apartment sale, underpriced everything I wanted to sell, and watched Amie's stuff slip away to people in the building, people off the street. Some people quibbled about paying a couple of bucks for one of those fifty-dollar

Calvin Klein or Act III shirts. Alphonse came, said a ceramic bowl was his, and I gave it to him. I sold a neighbor Amie's piano cheap and her couch for ten bucks. I gave her friends anything they wanted, but they didn't want much. They were in, looking, whispering, and then out. We kept a few pieces of jewelry, two handbags, half a dozen sweaters, this and that, and at the end of the day brought in the Salvation Army to haul away the last remnants of my sister's property.

My hands, from touching all the material for four days, lost all of their skin oils and I contracted a severe case of eczema. For three months they scaled and itched, and I obsessively applied one of several salves two or three times a day, rubbing them hard into my hands, over and over again. Finally my skin grew moist again.

12

A RELUCTANT PUBLISHER

After I had been teaching for four years I saw I was sliding deeper and deeper into debt. I needed a second job and was qualified for nothing. Beyond that, I was restless and did not want to be defined by any one thing I did. I wanted to be a man, with diverse talents and desires, not only a teacher, a man who was finding some other things he could do reasonably well.

My first publishing interview was with the editor of a skin magazine. I got the man's name from my stepfather; I remembered, from summer work at the insurance brokerage, that he had a few clients with the words "publisher" or "publication" in their corporate name. I knew no one else who had any connection to that world. The editor's office walls were papered with overlapping photographs of women who lacked clothes and preferred contortionist positions. The man himself weighed at least four hundred pounds, had thin hair greased and flat against his skull, and dressed like a thrift shop, with an unsnugged tie; as I entered, he deftly putted a golf ball thirty feet across his office rug and into a device shaped like a vagina.

I thought of my four small children and all the unpaid bills and dunning threats, and of Austin Warren, the great ascetic scholar under whom I had written my doctoral dissertation on an obscure New England poet who believed that his poems had been dictated to him by the Holy Spirit. So committed was Jones Very to this belief that when Emerson, who edited the first collection of Very's poems, wanted to change a letter here, a comma there, Very refused to let him do so. The poems were not his to change. This led the great dry Transcendentalist to utter one of his rare witticisms: "Cannot the Spirit parse and spell?" Since my dissertation was an edition of Very's poems, I had wrestled for many months with the same errant dictation from the Divine Afflatus.

I had been a full-time professor of English at Hunter College for several years and I now needed a second job. I was mad for literature and lit by the prospect of sharing my passion with the young for the rest of my life; I did not consider giving up the classroom—nor did I for more than twenty years. But I was desperate. Jones Very might think that "The hand and foot that stir not, they shall find / Sooner than all the rightful place to go," but I needed a job sooner than that and a more aggressive approach to salvation. Still, the skin route was too bumpy for me. I could not do it. Randomly, I decided that regular trade-book publishing—if I could squeeze open a door—was probably a wiser compromise.

I had no book or editing experience, and no knowledge of who published what, so in the Hunter College library I simply made a list of 103 book publishers and wrote to all of them. Only Herbert Michelman, editor in chief at Crown Publishers, responded. He told me I could start the next day on a two-week trial. On the third Wednesday, a few days beyond the trial period, I met him in the men's bathroom, asked if I was supposed to stay on; he nodded, and I did, for sixteen years. The first thing I noted about this book publishing was that *Rebel Rookie* and *The Negligent Doctor* were not Melville. I felt like an outsider then and still had a touch of that feeling when I left the publishing world decades later. Though I had the Wharton degree, I was far from a natural businessman; my switch to literature, and ten years of obsessive reading, may have seen to that. And my critical affections lay with older works; frankly, I never grew comfortable with that odd tug between author and editor, across the range of talent. At Crown I was assigned a manuscript by a famous general's son who would not change one of a hundred lines like his unforgettable "And then they began the foreplay." He was the supreme example of absolute artistic integrity without a trace of talent, almost as if he (like Jones Very) believed that someone more important had dictated the book.

Crown was a freewheeling arena and I tried to make a place for myself in it, and within the industry, rewriting a lot of the mediocre books that came the company's way in those days, trying to learn this new trade, find worthwhile books from the unsolicited piles and from agents, edit with the hand of Arthur pulling the sword from the stone, save authors from themselves and maximize their strengths and find the best way of bringing them into the world; I also wanted a list all mine and chose the little specialized world of fly-fishing, about which I had remained passionate. Every afternoon at five-ten, so I could get to my five-forty class, I'd race from West Eighteenth Street up to Hunter, though once a term, as if I were in a Kafka parable, the Lexington Avenue subway skipped Sixty-eighth and Seventy-seventh streets and stopped at Eighty-sixth, and my classroom would be empty by the time I got there. I held both jobs full-time for sixteen years, became full professor and executive editor, and managed to write ten books of my own and several hundred articles during that period. Somehow I also ghostwrote, first page to last, four books at nights and on weekends.

What energy I had then.

CROWN WAS RUN by Nat Wartels, the founder, who had a cherubic face, white hair, and a desk notorious for its mountains of papers on which he left old checks, contracts, orders, legal briefs, lit cigarettes, and whatnot else. He could pluck what he needed from a pile without hesitation; one pile, several feet high, was pockmarked with cigarette burns. He had begun as Outlet Books, buying remainder stock from other publishers, and when the remaindered books sold well at the lower prices, he reprinted them as Bonanza, promotional books in hardcover. Then he began original publishing at Crown, with the fail-safe backup of being able to remainder to himself for two dollars a book that had cost him one dollar to produce. One day, at an editorial meeting, when someone said a book would eventually make a terrific promotional reprint, the editor David McDowell remarked, in his great southern drawl, "Crown still sucks the hind teat of Bonanza Books."

Nat would buy up failed or failing small presses over lunch, use them for tax write-offs, sell off a few titles, remainder a lot, put a few into the Crown line. In the bowels of one Crown warehouse were the residues of some of the great moribund small publishers, Covici-Friede; Howell, Soskin; Derrydale; and many others. Clark Potter's company, Clarkson N. Potter, he kept, and it eventually flourished and is now a strong, distinct part of Random House; Clark once told me that with everything else he had lost—his inheritance, the family's salt farm in Rhode Island—he'd also lost the use of his name for the rest of his life. When I started my own house, I always had that graveyard in mind as a destiny to avoid like a toxic swamp. Nat was a hard negotiator, quietly ruthless with innocent authors, and I once had to tell the teenage Leonard Maltin to get a good lawyer; the tough lawyer-agent Mort Janklow called Nat one of the nicest, fairest guys in book publishing, but that's like asking a wolf to comment on another wolf, and not asking the opinion of the rabbit.

When I became executive editor, jacket copy for a new Robin Moore book came across my desk and I saw this heading on the back cover: "People Are Saying . . ." and then a series of short modest comments, like "The best war novel since *War and Peace*," "No one since Hemingway understands courage better," "Robin Moore captures the emotions so well that he reminds me of William Shakespeare." I went into Nat's office and said I didn't think we should put the jacket through without confirming the sources of these comments. He frowned. He said I should put it through as typeset. He said, "I'm a people, aren't I?" A "word-of mouth book" was one of his favorite marketing campaign slogans. An author who had published half a dozen books with Crown told me, "By this he means: an underling takes a copy of the book out the back door of the Avenel warehouse, waves it around for thirty seconds, and if no one starts talking puts it back on the shelf."

I'd edited a fishing book by Robert Traver, a.k.a. John Voelker, the great judge who wrote *Anatomy of a Murder*, and when he told me that Hemingway's sister Sunny was a friend and that she had a manuscript about her brother but hated New York and would not send it to me, Nat said, "Fly out and grab it." The old judge, already pickled in bourbon at noon, drove us from the airport in Petoskey to the famous Hemingway family cottage on Walloon Lake, near which most of the Nick Adams stories are centered. It was a clear, sharp October day, with the poplars bright yellow, and I recognized the place at once; I even saw the initials "EH" carved into the outhouse door. No more than a minute after I met her, Sunny said, "John, I want to speak with you!" They went outside together and I heard Sunny's brash cold voice say, "He's a Jew," and then the good liberal judge's quiet reassuring tones. She was a deliciously awful person—large, mannish, with big breasts, a straight back, and overactive arrogant glands—and she kept, as the unifying design motif in her house, hundreds of plastic and porcelain fornicating frogs. In midafternoon she grabbed a shotgun and fired point-blank at a fellow running his motor-boat too fast, too near the dock. She had typed *A Farewell to Arms* but was not shy of admitting that she had not read it or anything else by her brother except the story "Soldier's Home," in which she was the "good sister." She had written only three or four pages of the alleged book (mostly arguing that Ernest had not slept with Prudence, the Ojibway girl, based on the irrefutable evidence that Pru would have told her), and toward the end of that long day she made a point of showing me a row of trees planted by her mother, Grace, at the birth of each of her six children. Two of them were now stumps. "Dutch elm?" I asked. "No," she said, "they were Ursula's and Marcelline's trees. We had a fight and I cut them down." The stumps, I think, were warnings. I can still see them, breaking the neat row, screaming.

Nat worked late; I called him that evening and said, "There's nothing here. And she's a flaming anti-Semite." Nat asked, "Does she have pictures?" When I told him that she had all the family photograph albums, including Ernest's, he said, "Get the photos, we'll make a book." *Ernie*—a name Hemingway despised—came out nine months later, and Crown got the new author an interview with Gene Shalit on the *Today* show. Sunny waited until the camera panned to her, then extracted from a large knitting bag a pair of scissors the size of pruning shears and advanced on Shalit, who lurched backward. She insisted on cutting off a lock of his curly hair for her friends back in Michigan before she'd say a word. The book proved Nat's theory that anything whatsoever about Van Gogh, sex, or Hemingway would make money: the dreadful little thing sold eighteen thousand copies.

AND THEN A press of my own.

Timothy Benn, a British publisher, came to me and asked if I would start a subsidiary for him in the colonies, to be called

Nick Lyons Books. I was still teaching full-time at Hunter, which had lately demanded that I go to consulting status with Crown. I began the little firm, with the British funding, on my dining room table, and called myself a consultant to myself. I signed a ten-book contract to produce books for Doubleday—as a "packager," a word I'd never heard before and did not much like. The books would all be in the field of outdoor leisure sport, primarily fly-fishing. I used freelancers for production matters and did everything else myself. I rarely met schedules, the books sold far fewer copies than the Doubleday computers had predicted they would sell, and four years later, when I had produced some fifty books for Doubleday, Winchester, Norton, and Schocken, I was about to quit, out of frustration with myself, the companies, the whole setup. Then Timothy Benn, chairman of the hundred-year-old Benn Group, was summarily discharged and I was advised that the subsidiary would be sold. I told the corporation's executives flatly that there was nothing to sell. The books had all been placed with publishers, I was the only asset, and I didn't put much value on myself and would not be sold.

Malcolm Lowe, a lay preacher in the Church of England, flew over to negotiate with me; he had instigated Timothy's dismissal. He was a tall, starchy man, darkly dressed, and put two small Bibles on the table when we began to negotiate. For support, I kept trotting out phantom accountants and lawyers who would not let me do this or that. In the end I bought myself cheap, which was what I was worth, along with two used desks, a beloved antique stapler, and the rights to a lot of books owned by others. I raised $100,000 from seven trusting friends with whom I had fished and they signed documents stating that they had a bundle of money and were prepared to lose all they'd invested. At the end of that first year, they nearly had. I had sent out a release after I became independent, quoting Jim in *Huckleberry Finn:* "I owns mysef, en I's wuth eight hund'd dollars." By the end of that year, the figure was less than zero. Welcome to independent publishing. All the old support systems from my Crown and Benn days were gone—receptionists, first readers, editorial committees, copy editors, designers, production wizards, marketing teams, salesmen, billers, a rights department, people to collect money and compute royalties and pay them, accountants, and a host of other experts. There was no one to tell me what to do, or how; there was no one to blame.

What to do? My friend Garth Battista, who runs Breakaway Books out of his home in Halcottsville, New York, does it all himself: editing, composition, design, all sales except trade distribution. I could not. I was over fifty and technologically a dinosaur. I had taken a junior partner, Peter Burford, and now hired an entry-level young Turk, Bill Wolfsthal, to do everything we did not want to do; I "unpackaged" myself by raising more money from some of those same trusting friends (one sent a check for $25,000 on his way to South America, with a note saying, "If you need more, call Joan"); and I bought back the fifty books I'd sold to other publishers—something few, if any, former packagers have done. I hired an outside sales consultant, who attached us to five sales rep groups, instead of using a distribution company, so we could control all sales; I built a team of freelancers to copyedit, proofread, and design, and got full-time employees for these positions as we could afford them. My daughter, Jenny, helped collect money and sold rights part-time. My sons, Paul, Charles, and Tony, helped as they could, usually arranging the endless index cards of potential accounts I kept obsessively for fifteen years. I didn't learn to use the computer until after I'd retired.

I saw at once that a small independent press was not just a small version of a big house but an entity all its own, and that all small presses are—or should be—sui generis. What, exactly, should Nick Lyons Books be?

I kept the focus on outdoor leisure sport, building what I thought was the country's finest fly-fishing list, partly on the assumption that I wanted to be better than the big houses in at least one area. When a fishing friend put me in touch with Rita Gam, the actress with the great name, I thought we might have a chance to spread our wings, become general trade publishers. Rita was in her late fifties, had acted only sporadically in recent years, and several times I made the mistake of introducing her as the star of *The Thief* with Ray Milland—"You know, that silent movie." She was a great blast of fresh air after all the Quill Gordons and No-Hackle Duns. We were able to get her onto the *Today* show not long after her former roommate, Grace Kelly, died in the car crash; she had a chapter on Grace in her book *Actress to Actress*. Jane Pauley had agreed not to ask Rita about Grace, but the third question was the big sandbag: Who had Grace slept with? Rita said politely that she would not comment about that. "Oh, come on," Pauley persisted, but Rita just smiled and steadfastly said no, winning my undying admiration. So thirty seconds into the interview, from the wings, I saw Pauley call for a break and then motion with her hand to have Rita hauled off with a crooked cane.

One of our first books was *Uneeda Review*, with the subtitle *Like a Hole in the Head*, a parody by Louis Rubin and William Harmon of a literary magazine. It featured an article by "Otis Sistrunk," the football player, called "The Poem as an Action of Field," and a poem by Emily Dickinson in the *Noron Reader* section that began, "The soul selects her own Sorority— / Then—shuts the Dorm—" Every graduate student in the country was sure to buy a copy. The ad on the back, for a writers' conference, proclaimed, "Work *Under* a Writer of Your Own Choice," and listed in bold type twenty famous literary figures who (as the footnote confessed in seven-point type) had been invited. "No hassles. No tension. No bad criticism," the ad continued. How could the book fail? We put a full-page advertisement in the *Publications of the Modern Language Association* and got precisely one order—from (bless her) Margaret Atwood. Despite a glowing *Publishers Weekly* review, the book got two minuscule notices nationwide and sold only 527 copies for an awful lot of work.

One of the sales reps told me that the world did not need another small general trade publisher, that we should stick to our niche; but we thought there was a way to segue into deeper waters and did so by seeking the lit'ry edges of the niche, where it bled into natural history, adventure, and personal memoir. It was exciting to find a dozen fine new—or almost new—young writers. We published David Quammen's *Natural Acts*, his first collection of natural history essays; Verlyn Klinkenborg's first book, *Making Hay*; W. D. Wetherell's *Vermont River*, which had been rejected by half a dozen publishers; Jon Krakauer's first book, *Eiger Dreams*; Janet Lembke's brilliant *River Time*; and Eddy L. Harris's edgy *Mississippi Solo*—the memoir of a young black man who (to paraphrase a friend of his) canoed the Mississippi from Minnesota, where no one had seen anyone who looked like him, through the South, where they wouldn't much like him.

It was exhilarating, and we found unique ways to sell so

many copies of such books that, in our third year, we got a front-page write-up in the *Wall Street Journal*, noting that no other publisher the writer had ever heard of could have sold a couple of dozen copies of a literary book called *Making Hay* through the NAPA Auto Parts store in Wayzata, Minnesota. Bill Wolfsthal, our brash young sales manager, had even gotten a Scribner's window display on Fifth Avenue, using four bales of hay he had bought up-country. He waited with a camera for something to happen, and, when a Hasid with a black hat and ringlets paused, puzzled, he got a photograph of the scene and sent it across the country with the caption "Oy, hay." The release and photograph were picked up by thirty-two newspapers.

Since I was the only person in the little house who knew that *Paraleptophlebia* was not a foot fungus, I read every manuscript even faintly connected to fly-fishing that came in. Sometimes there were as many as a few hundred a year; you would have thought that everyone who ever cast a line had a book in his creel. I once even had a fellow wade out to me in the middle of the Yellowstone River with a telltale manila envelope in his hands and have long regretted that I didn't just say, "Oops," and drop it in the drink. My daughter, who became a fine literary agent, was once given an opportunity to look at a manuscript for a seven-hundred-page novel by her dentist, who had a nasty little power tool in his hand at the time. Her mouth wide open, she could only nod painfully; it was an offer she could not refuse. Once I said, in a long front-page article I wrote for the *New York Times Book Review*, that I read everything that came my way myself and always tried to make a helpful comment or two. What a dumbbell! I traced hundreds of manuscripts to that article, and I was unable to accept even one. Though we paid minute advances, a number of agents came to us with books they couldn't place elsewhere. I remember the late John Cushman apologizing profusely for sending me *Bear Attacks: Their Causes and Avoidance*, by Stephen Herrero, a friend of one of his best authors, a man with a dying son. No one would have it. We were his last hope. It was a splendid book on the subject and we eventually sold more copies of it than there are bears in the universe. Ted Hoagland wrote me that I had done more to harm bears than anyone in history. I told him I thought otherwise but published or republished nearly a dozen of *his* books.

THE ESSENTIAL INGREDIENT for a small house to flourish is the list of books it chooses to publish, and the strength of NLB, which became Lyons & Burford and then the Lyons Press, was always our particular mix of books. Part of our strategy had always been to republish older books, in a mulch with the best practical and literary books we could find. Our accountant recommended a 1950s book, long out of print, called *The Long Walk*, by Slavomir Rawicz, a Polish lieutenant who escaped from a Soviet gulag with six others and walked across the Gobi Desert and over the Himalayas. At last count the Lyons Press had sold 275,000 copies of the old book and it had been optioned for the movies twice. We republished six flagrantly anthropomorphic 1950s books by the naturalist John Crompton, long forgotten by the world, got major reviews, and went through five or six printings of each. Half a dozen old fly-fishing authors got new lives when we published their books after they had been remaindered decades earlier, which made me feel we could do that uniquely: conserve good books, rarely remainder any, keep them in print until the next flood. We learned dozens of strategies for resurrecting such books and for keeping them in print, at a time when larger houses were told by accountants to clean the bins every six months.

Suddenly we were a business with fifteen or sixteen employees, who depended on us for a paycheck, and—except for that first year, miraculously—we were always profitable. Our accountant, Dick Frieden—the old loyal roommate of mine from Penn—flew in seven times a year from California to handle our financial matters; he explained cash flow to this aging English professor, and the need for inventory control, and taxes, telling me why you could have a profit and no money in the bank to pay the IRS, which would not accept its cut in copies of *Uneeda Review*. He told me why a great small press like North Point, which had two best sellers (*West with the Night* and *Son of the Morning Star*), could lose more than $1 million a year on gross sales of only several million and eventually be unsalable; how expanding on the assumption that these best sellers could fund future growth, then not having additional best sellers to take their place, and, as a double whammy, getting the great tide of returns could be fatal. "But they do wonderful books," I protested, and he merely smiled an accountant's knowing smile.

It was Dick who helped my son Tony, a lawyer, who had asked if he could come into the firm and had then done some sales, some general office work. Tony grew bored and restless and Dick said I should put him in charge of the money. I was terrified but did—and Tony flourished.

Outdoor leisure sport expanded for us to include all sports and natural history and then literary essays faintly related to natural history and sport, which led to books on all up-country matters and cooking, gardening, crafts, adventure, climbing, camping, horses, dogs, collecting, fitness, art, homesteading, western affairs, and much else, in a kind of constellation of loose niches that had some unity, at least to me, even with the inclusion of three books of poetry and a growing number of novels. I did not do another book of poetry but kept growing our number of novels. I did not publish another book by an actress, nor another literary parody, but by the time a big-time agent snubbed me by referring to another house as being *real* publishers, we were publishing eighty books a year, had four or five hundred in print, and most niches blurred into general trade.

We kept refining our host of cheap, pinpointed, aggressive, obsessive marketing techniques, and they worked—most of the time. I wrote thousands of personal letters on my Underwood Standard typewriter, to reviewers and dealers and wholesalers and columnists and auto-parts stores. I decided to take on more books at a time when most houses were doing fewer—to develop new areas, spread our risk, have more books that earned a little money and the chance that a few might earn a lot. It was not a tight, uniformly distinguished list, but every list had a few fine new authors, and we became solidly profitable; at a time when the major publishers were earning 1 or 2 percent net profit, if any, we regularly earned 15 to 26 percent.

The problem with fine new authors, of course, whose stock you have pushed so high, is that they are often ambitious fine new authors. It is gut-wrenching: you write endless letters to the world, saying, "We're publishing this brilliant young author. You don't know him yet but he is the most . . . and the . . . and is sure to be the next . . ." and then you get good sales and have the prominent reviews come in—earned by the book itself, but perhaps not overlooked because of your letters—and you grow a bit jittery but remain confident because face-to-face and in a dozen letters he promised to stand with you until he drops— and then, *poof*, they're gone. One agent said they were going to hold out paperback rights to her young genius's next book. After a day or so I decided, Well, at least we have the hardcover of this bright fellow we've urged from obscurity, and I called to say, "Okay, it's a lousy thing but . . ." and she said that she and her boy had decided to pull the hardcover, too. I never heard from the man again. He was a great writer—he might at least have written me a brief note.

Several went to Knopf; Jon Krakauer went on to much higher things; several never looked back; a few did; "out of courtesy," one had his new agent send me his proposal after the auction for his second book was over. Friends said I should be proud of my eye; I should understand. And I did. But it hurt like hell being merely the first-book publisher, the perpetual stepping-stone, the Danny Rose. Years later, an editor at a large house told my daughter that he always watched our list carefully for authors to swipe, and he in fact poached two. Young employees we'd trained from their first days in publishing left, too, for the big places, the bigger game.

Against all that, we found many prominent authors, mature and at the height of their fame, who were happy to publish with us—not their primary work, perhaps, but smaller books about their passions. Tom McGuane did a wonderful book for us on horses, Jay McInerney one on his fascination for wine; we republished Le Anne Schreiber's haunting *Midstream* and her original *Light Years*; we published Ted Hoagland's *Tigers & Ice* and a spate of his older essay collections. We did fifty or sixty of these, including old and new books by John Graves, Joy Williams, Rick Bass, Gavin Maxwell, George Plimpton, Niko Tinbergen, S. J. Perelman, Richard Ellis, and a host of others including a wonderful memoir by a rural Montana doctor named Ron Losee; *Doc* elicited a plea from *Publishers Weekly* for Losee to be cloned, since the world needed more doctors like him. Some, like the McGuane, sold exceptionally well, and all brought us the kind of broad, serious attention of which a small publisher can never get enough.

AND THEN SUDDENLY I was sixty-five, with two brand-new titanium hips, spooked by an exploded gallbladder, my young partner announcing that he'd like to start his own house, and my memory beginning to slip. I told an old friend to write me a severe letter about the shipping problems he'd had with us, that I'd circulate it to the appropriate people. I completely forgot our conversation, and then, a month or so later, I received a savage letter from him complaining of this and that shipping mishap. I got livid. I dashed off a more savage letter to him, asking him where he got off, after our long and cordial friendship, writing me a letter like that. He did not respond. Then, a full week or so later, I vaguely remembered.

When one author, after three years of delays, during which time he'd written a couple of books for other publishers, submitted a book called *Life List*, about all the birds he'd seen in his lifetime, and there were only a couple of dozen birds treated, I blew up. "Well, let's say it's half a book," he quipped, "so I'll only take half the advance." My nerves had frayed and I was increasingly ill-tempered and caustic, and I shouted back that he'd better get a lawyer; no one would buy half a bridge.

Our art director came in one day and blithely told me, "The bad news is that we've lost two sheets of original slides from a stock photo house and they've billed us for eighty-six thousand dollars. But the good news," she said brightly, "is that we have five years to pay." My solution to that problem at that time would have been to go out for a second lunch. But Tony had grown swiftly into his work and was a lawyer. So I turned the problem over to him. Two days later he told me it was all resolved: it was their fault; and he had found a way to bill *them* for a couple thousand dollars. I quickly calculated that the difference between us was $88,000 plus the cost of a second lunch. And he regularly saved me from my greatest nemesis: one too many authors with an ego as big as the Ritz, writers who would never die of unrequited self-love. So I turned the business over to him and crossed my fingers.

I did so even after a dozen friends sternly warned me to reread *King Lear* carefully before making my decision final. Tony was different and forceful and sales-driven, and I knew I would have to let him have his head. After a few feeble efforts to do otherwise, I sat back and rooted for him and the company—and, like a good old father, didn't speak unless spoken to.

The rest of the Lyons Press story is his to tell someday, but after a couple of years I felt less like Lear than Anchises, carried from the sacked city of Troy on the shoulders of his son, Aeneas. Tony published two hundred books a year, quadrupled the size of the business in three years, increased its profitability, and then negotiated a decent sale of the company.

Some months after the sale I called Bruce Harris, an old friend from my Crown days and then president of Workman

Publishing, and he said, "Ah, it's Nick Lyons, the man who did everything wrong and came up with the roses."

And so, sixty years have passed since I brooded about a poorly schooled Holy Spirit and whether my fate had to include all those nude young women in erotic poses. I was a reluctant publisher to the end but was always intrigued by the parliament of skills needed for the task. It was exciting and freewheeling, as far from academia as you could get, nerve-racking, earthy, and robust. It also required a good measure of luck. Much of the time I seriously doubted I could survive. So many small independent book publishers don't, though I am convinced that they are the hope of the industry. I can't think that anything I remembered from Wharton helped, but I took some satisfaction in learning how rewarding one part of the business world could be, and how I'd come half circle.

What intrigues me most as I think about those years, in the classroom and then in the publishing world, was how both teaching and publishing hauled me out of myself, invited me to consider the work, the person in class or behind the typewriter or in the office. The skills I'd learned could help a student or an author's life. I became part of a larger family, part of a moral universe. I had not sacrificed but I had shared, and with pleasure I still share, and it is an extension of who I've become.

But perhaps the most exciting part of publishing books was discovering in a just-opened envelope words that danced and wisdom I could bet would last. Never a Melville, but some of it has.

13

MARI, MONTANA, THE SPHINX, AND ME

With money we received from the sale of the Lyons Press, Mari and I began a life not of leisure but of intense concentration on our painting and writing; and we traveled every year to Paris, Madrid, Venice, Florence, and walked everywhere and spent long days in the great museums. I also managed to fish intently again. The period lasted nearly two decades and so many of the places and events became so much a part of us that I think of them in some sort of enduring present tense.

From the house on the bench, I can see Sphinx Mountain rise from a low section of the Madison Range like a gargantuan stump, rudely cut. It is the farthest solid thing across the lush bottomland, beyond the ribbon that is the Madison River, cobalt blue between the cottonwoods. Now and then, on a bright morning, with the sun rising beyond it, the river is polished silver. Beyond the river there is another bench, then the sloping foothills, then the strange mountain itself, fourth in line from the north, after Fan, Lone, and Cedar. Today there is a solid pack of snow in what appears to be its concave top, veins of white in the front crevice, a washboard grid of snow on the left side, with palisades above. We have been here for two weeks and I have never seen this particular Sphinx. Today it looks cupped at the top, like a vessel about to receive something, though I don't think anyone upstairs is handing anything out lately, if in fact he hasn't departed to other worlds, we having made a mess of things here. From the bench I can make out a couple of wood or metal bridges, jackleg fence posts, a bit of barbed wire, a cedar cabin.

As we drove along the rutted dirt road from Ennis the first day of our summer visit, it was at first not visible, then partially visible, then visibly different each moment, constantly changing into a procession of configurations and colors. It seems in perpetual motion, like the Montana clouds, symbols of mutability. In various lights it was variously dark green at its base from pines that weld it to the rising hills; then Payne's gray at its rocky summit, or slate gray, or purple, or white, or pink, or ochre—or, yesterday afternoon, tawny red. The earth's anatomy is exposed here—sinew and bone of what holds it, the trees a skin. Some folks in town say they used to call it Red Mountain or Brick Top; someone said it once looked like a Sphinx, but a piece fell off. No one knows exactly when people started to call it that.

Several times I woke early, about five, and sat naked at the window watching the emergence of the sun; at first the top of the Sphinx is not there and I must take it on trust that it still *is* because it was. It is *always* there, I must remind myself, even when it is not visible; what matters matters, whether it's perceived or not. Then, inchmeal, it incarnates, as the brightening behind the dun-gray clouds allows it to become itself, and then suddenly the sun and mountain are so bright that, for a moment, I must look away. And sometimes in the evenings, with the infection of light from the sunset in the west, above the Gravellies, it is a dozen gaudy reds and purples, even bright crimson, as if it contains fire, as in a Turner. And sometimes it is merely a silhouette, a cutout, a straight man to the sky— black clouds, pink light, streaks of blue.

The mountain changes as you look at it, and it changes radically as we drive south on Route 287 toward West Yellowstone, or float the river, or wander down along the Madison Valley bottomland. Two miles south and that structure in front, called the Helmet, begins to walk away and we can see clearly that there are two mountains, not one, substantially apart. In a photograph friends from Big Sky sent me, of the other side of the mountain, it bears no resemblance to what my eyes tell me it is from the bench; our son Paul, standing on the narrow ledge at its summit, looked out for fifty miles in all directions along the Madison River but saw little of the thing he stood upon.

Wandering and changing as it does the mountain makes me think of Melville's whale, ubiquitous in time and space, here, there, spotted in several places at the same time, well out of water here in the Rockies.

But this heap of stone is dead. It does not breathe, does not seek anyone; nor is it sought for oil or vengeance, though the real estate brokers have begun to hawk its image. It is merely there in front of us, big as life, solid as a fire in a cave in the

Caucasus, different on Tuesday after the high snows came, and ten minutes ago, now that the snow is melting, perfectly indifferent to my eyes, without inherent meaning, dumb as stone— a mass of reddish rock, coarse gravel, and red sand eponymously called Sphinx conglomerate, originally under water, then formed seventy million years ago. And even now this anchor of the landscape is not quite fixed. Gradually, it has been forced upward by geological forces similar to those that caused the huge earthquake forty miles south in 1959. Some geologists claim it still grows by as much as two inches a year.

I am not a geologist and can never know more than a faction of its life—not even what they mean when they say it is "clearly contemporaneous with Laramide regional deformation," which sounds like art criticism—and that second- or third-hand. But I am here on the bench and it is always there, across the valley, and it intrigues me and it has been trying for some weeks to wedge itself into my brain, become more than it is—though of course it is I who am trying to make a heap of rock become more than it is, and I have to remember Freud's observation that sometimes a cigar is just a cigar. Still, Emerson says, "Every object rightly seen unlocks a new faculty of the soul," and this hunk is worth the looking, getting into my head.

Mari is here too, of course, and for her it simply begs to be painted. It is an object, like many others she has painted, that serves merely as an object from which to begin, like Cézanne's apples or his Mont Sainte-Victoire, which also are themselves and more. And it is various enough for her to view in many different ways. She has painted it from the valley, where I go to fish in a spring creek, from upriver and down, and from our house, directly across. It reminds her of Goya's architect—and

Rembrandt's late self-portraits, and Mount Fuji, and Cézanne's mountain in Provence.

Today, from my table in the living room, I watch Mari sketch in the first tentative outline of the mountain. She is using Mars brown and a thin brush. First I see the Sphinx, in front of me, in itself, steadily emerge from the canvas. Then there is blue, which is also sky, and strokes that are trees or fields or the far bench.

In two hours there are greens that might be cottonwoods, a dozen yellows and greens that are the valley that sits between our house and the river, with hints of blue flax and lupine. I see patches of cobalt blue, streaks of silver, and look beyond the canvas to a river, visible between the trees, the only moving thing in the landscape other than the hawk hunting above the field. What's on the canvas does not "depict" or "represent" but has become some strange new creature of its own. The rose brambles in front of me are not on the canvas, nor is the white-tailed deer in the valley, nor the hawk (now gone, anyway), nor a thousand other details. But those forms on the canvas could not exist without that other thing, the physical thing, beyond it. This that is on the canvas is not an emotional response either, an "echo of the soul"; nor is it romantic. I shall learn what it is, I promise myself.

I LOOK AT the woman now, tall and thin, her hair frizzy and blond, in a tank top and blue coveralls, separate from me now, caught in some triangle with landscape and canvas, and I can see what she sees (with my different eyes), and I can see that thing on the canvas, struggling to become itself. A camera would capture it all, all at once, the Sphinx at this moment, as it has been for the past few hours. The mountain will be different again before she stops painting for the day. There are great photographs and she knows it, but she cursed the camera impishly yesterday when I suggested that it could anchor the scene for her, become a point of reference.

"Different mountain," she said. Then: "I love photographs as much as anyone, dear, especially if they're of our children."

So, we have come to this spot to transact some private business—I to fish and write, Mari to put color and forms in watercolor and oil paint on paper and canvas. We'll be here a month, maybe more, and perhaps we'll come back. We are not of this place but of a place that is a totem for placelessness, a city—a rootless nowhere, full of jewels. We both want a somewhere—but we are visitors here, and at this time of our lives we fear that we may never have such a place. This is not Walden Pond; but we are here together, after a trip of nearly forty years' duration, over rocky terrain, with four children, now grown. And this is a *place*, and the mountain is real—though it may well also be a state of mind.

My Underwood Standard, Model S, vintage 1945, is on the table before me. I have transported to this place heaps of books, notebooks, and paper; I have thirty years' worth and I need to organize them—and my life. I have my fly rods and innumerable boxes of flies stacked in the hallway. My boots and vest hang on nails just outside the front door.

I don't understand my passion for fishing, and especially for the brown trout; nor do I have to. But it is there, and Vaughan is due at the house in an hour to take us downriver.

Suddenly, that is immensely important to me.

YOU CAN SEE the great mountain now and then as we float in the late afternoon on the Madison River—between the trees, across the fields, towering over the benches, here, then gone, but we have come for something else this time. The Sphinx is incidental, irrelevant.

When we first came to the Downing House, three weeks ago, the giant stoneflies had begun to hatch and all day, every day, cars towing drift boats rattled up and down the Varney Road, throwing dust. There were fifty-three of them one day and that was more than I cared to contend with. Floaters came down the ribbon of cobalt regularly, and because of the low willows, you could not always see the boat; sometimes it looked as if they were walking or sitting on water as they glided swiftly downriver. The river, which was high when we arrived, has been dropping by degrees; I walk to it every day, look over the Varney Bridge, watch the rocks appear with greater distinctness, a world more visible each hour the river clears. And as it clears, now and then, I can spot the wavering dark forms of the trout.

I fished it a few times from one of the access points and now, finally, I am floating with Vaughan, casting quickly to one bank or the other, watching a big fly float along the shadow line near the shore, where I've always found the largest fish. It is pleasant work. I stand in the front, leaning into the concave nose of the McKenzie boat, and watch the water come to me and search for likely places to cast, perhaps a rising fish. There are absolutely no fish rising and I have the odd feeling that their numbers have somehow diminished. There are more birds. Earlier, an osprey dive-bombed the river with extended claws, smashing into the riffled surface and coming up with a two-pound rainbow trout, gleaming silver, still shaking as the great bird lifted off—one fish the better of me.

Mari does not fish but she is showing more interest in this intense dance of mine—leaning forward, the hard look, the poised rod, the angle of the line being cast, the strike, the struggle. She is watching me at my play, and out of the corner of my eye I watch her. Several times when we stopped floating I merely sat back on a rock to her side and kept glancing at her working, the quick strokes of her watercolor brush—like a swallow inscribing a shadow on the flat surface of the creek—fixing an image on the paper, not the scene itself but some painted adumbration, some other world, separate and complete unto itself, hooked to the real one. Watercolor painting had been new to her when we first went west fifteen years ago, and at first she worked as if her medium were still oil paint, which she could paint over, rework, build, even as Albert Ryder worked his haunting scenes into brooding layers of darkness. Watercolor was quick and final.

But on the river, my eyes always returned to moving water, with those great speckled mysteries holding somewhere in its depths. Then Mari vanished, the mountain was gone, and I was concerned only with how to get my fly into the long shadow against the shoreline, beyond the current seam, and how to manipulate the line and fly so that the fly would stay in that dark shadow and float naturally. This was a modest goal. It was not nearly like trying to get some fragment of the Montana landscape onto a piece of paper or canvas without competing with a camera or a realist. But though I was always up to my gills in the first, increasingly I realized how much I wanted to understand the other. For I love painting and for forty years, watching Mari's work evolve, it has been a deeper and deeper part of my life. She never quit, despite the indifference, the raw discouragement, even from her closest friends—like Cézanne took it from Zola in *The Masterpiece*. She was never slick or satisfied; she looked, she struggled, she grew, and I loved her work, which had since I married her been entangled with my life.

At the end of the float I helped Vaughan trailer the boat, and then he drove us back to the Downing House. Mari had made half a dozen sketches and she laid them out on the dining table and we looked carefully at each. One was a happy little rendering of a boat going by; another was muddy and she summarily ripped it up—watercolor admits no possibility of revision, the sort of tinkering Yeats and Flaubert were given to, fussing with a line for a week or a month, until the result seemed "a moment's thought." We once visited a famous watercolorist's studio and saw engraved into a beam a maxim: "Fixing a watercolor is like trying to change a lie: the more you try the worse it gets." There was a quick sketch of the brown I caught, animated, wavering in the water, sure-handed, and one from the back of the McKenzie River boat, past Vaughan, who had rowed, including the nose of the boat and a bit of me. At my weight I was glad she had not been able to record all of me in the sketch. There were two drawings that included the mysterious mountain, poking through the trees. That was the metamorphosis of it: a thing outside of her, with a life of its own, like a brown trout, finding its way into her notebooks and then, perhaps, becoming a painting or, like the one of me and the famous British flyfisher, John Goddard, ending up on the cover of a book. Or, like the muddy sketch, it gets ripped. "I don't paint to keep from spoiling paper or canvas," she liked to say.

Mari's "fishing" had been better than mine, and it was better still when we tramped around Spring Creek a few days later, me fishing hard, she trailing me with pad, watching and sketching.

Mostly I forgot that she was there.

I fished up the familiar East Branch, knowing exactly how best to approach each pool, having a trim box of flies in my vest, the products of some mastery since, a decade earlier, I first blundered around this tough river. I enjoyed having developed the skills to fish here with some success. I took fish at the Middle Bend Pool and the Second Bend Pool and then, oblivious to all but the hypnotic tug of the river, I approached the Third Bend Pool. It was the smallest of the pools on the East Branch, with a sharp center current, several braided currents, a full 120-degree turn, and, beyond the currents, a slack eddy the size of a child's wading pool. The trick, I'd learned a few years ago, was to fish up the left side, the outer rim of the current, and directly upstream into the slack water. Too many anglers tried to fish across the current; I'd given that up years ago. Best was to stand very quietly against the left bank, the slack water no more than thirty feet above, and wait. That's what I did and in a few moments I saw a bit of nervous water that, in another context, might have meant a tadpole or a small turtle. It wasn't much. But I'd seen such movement here before. I cast a small Elk-Hair Caddis up to where the water had flounced a bit and a great buster of a brown trout took the fly at once, raced powerfully upriver, came caterwauling out of the water and crashing back, leaped again, and landed in a patch of thistles along the bank. "Ha!" I muttered, never having seen this before. For an instant I thought it might be trapped in the weeds, so I lifted myself onto the bank and prepared to race toward the great fish—perhaps six pounds of it—but the thrashing and flopping continued and the trout was soon back in the water, leaving my fly a scarred bit of feathers among the prickly leaves.

"Ahhhh," I said and turned to see if Mari had witnessed this dramatic clownishness.

But she was still sitting on the rim of the Middle Bend Pool, where I'd last seen her, an hour earlier.

WHEN I FIRST hauled Mari to Montana, decades ago, to fish this perfectly remarkable spring creek, she went reluctantly. She hated to leave her studio for a month and thought her oils and canvases too cumbersome to take along. Also, after far too many years of it, she still found the endless fish talk boring in the extreme and never tried to learn the difference between a *Hexagenia limbata* and a handsaw; and she still called my fly rods "poles."

But by the second year she began to work her way, increasingly, into the special demands of watercolor—and then, steadily, she began to paint almost as long as I fished, which is a lot. She'd set up her portable easel, low to the ground and out of the wind, sit on the canvas bush chair she'd brought, and get to work at once, finding fixed points in the vast Montana landscape to paint over and over, especially that certain stump of a form on the horizon. Or she'd trail after me, sketching with a pen, sometimes brushing color into the sketches. When I finished my book about this patch of water, I found a watercolor of a man crouched and casting that made a fine jacket, and I found forty line drawings that the publisher happily took for the interior. Our work commingled, and I realized too that she had finally made her connection to this odd and enduring passion of mine for rivers and fly-fishing, through her own work.

ONCE, ON A cold and drizzly evening after I'd fished hard all day, she insisted we go back to the river. I said I found it very comfortable in front of the fire, thank you. She asked if I was sick or something and I reluctantly allowed myself to be hauled down to the water. It was grayer and colder by Spring Creek and I sat in the driver's seat, warmly dressed, and took out a book while she started a small watercolor.

"You *are* sick, aren't you?" she said.

"Tired. Fished out," I said.

"That'll be the day."

"It's true."

"If you're not sick, get out of here and fish!" she said, and practically pushed me out of the car. I reluctantly took my rod down from the carrier on the roof of the Suburban, walked to the edge of the water, a vast pool, and shivered. I turned back to her and she pointed to a bright double rainbow near Sphinx Mountain. I smiled pleasantly, shivered and shook a few times, looked across the dark, cold water, saw a robust snout poke up some forty feet out, and took it on my first cast, the largest brown I've ever taken, which she sketched before I turned it back.

And then I said: "Satisfied?"

"No."

"Then let's go back to bed, big girl."

TWO THOUSAND MILES from here, there is a great gray city, called "Mannahatta" by Whitman, "parochial" and worse by western-ers I know. A dozen up-country friends have been conned within minutes of arriving at Grand Central Terminal, or blasted in the eyes by soot. One man would not get into a cab without an escort. In more than thirty-five years, I was mugged once, when a mob of kids surrounded Mari and me; one ripped off her necklace, and they scattered; and a quick hand got money from my pocket in the subway once. I try to keep three steps ahead of them now.

Two thousand miles from here, Mari has a large studio over H & H Bagels on Eightieth Street and Broadway. I think of her room often, with its hundreds and hundreds of paint-ings, books everywhere, still lifes with flowers, fruits, sculptor's props, and skulls she began to collect when her father, a California cattle rancher, sent her boxes labeled "Bones." And there are cityscapes, figure studies, dancers, early landscapes from the days we spent in Woodstock, and a great number of self-portraits, from all periods of her life, at least one painted on every birthday. In the room, I must slip sideways through the maze of canvases; I like to see brushes held on corrugated cardboard, paints fresh on wax paper, work in various stages of incarnation, mirrors, paint-stained coveralls, photographs and prints pinned to bits of wall space, bottles of damar varnish and turpentine; I like the thick smell of paint.

These past few years there are also large landscapes, made from the sketches and drawings of Montana, canvases up to seven by eight feet, perhaps thirty of them. When I enter this world I see the fullness of work, the mystery of art, a richness of spirit; some visitors are overwhelmed by the sheer volume of color and form, the canvases stacked face out, one enjambed with another, the room often dominated by one current series, like the new paintings of Montana.

After the most difficult years with our closely bunched kids, she rented a space on the third floor of this building, sharing it with a succession of painters and finally taking it all for herself, about a thousand square feet of it. A year ago she stretched out even further and took a storage room, to leave herself more space to paint.

Before these paintings of the Montana landscape, she did an extended series of self-portraits, and before that she did city-scapes and still lifes—fifty or more of each. The self-portraits, she told me the other night when we were looking out at the silhouette of the Sphinx, lit by a quarter moon, began because she had a cheap model. But they became a searching in paint for an elusive selfhood—intense, questing. "My self-portraits," she said, "frighten people, I think—women as well as men. An angry woman painted by a man—Dubuffet, de Kooning, Picasso—is an icon; an angry woman painted by a woman is intimidating, is a hag."

"But they're not angry," I argued.

"They're serious—and that's worse. It makes people very nervous."

MARI HAS ALWAYS painted. At age fifteen she heard that Max Beckmann was giving a summer course at Mills College, lied to her parents, saying that she was taking a swimming program, and every night wet her bathing suit and wrapped it up in a damp towel. Beckmann looked and said, *"Gut, gut, mein Kind,"* and pointed and nodded, and his wife, Quappi, translated a few words, and at the end of the summer she brought her parents to a room at the college that Beckmann had filled with her first paintings. And now, even after the fire destroyed all her early work, she has a thousand canvases and twice as many drawings and watercolors in that great room, two thousand miles from here, above H & H Bagels.

It is a rainy day and Mari is painting her Big Enigma, a brown hump like the mountain, me. She painted me, nearly forty years ago, naked, in college. She was always partial to cheap models who did not have to be flattered—herself, me—and I was cheap as dirt, thin then, and would sit for a smile though I couldn't hold the pose for three minutes.

Now I am a mountain of a man, graying by the hour, but I can sit for days, reading or fussing with a few sentences. Mari says under her breath that I have everything her regular models have, only more of it.

As I sit here in front of the window, still as Buddha or the Sphinx, where she can see the old mountain over my left shoulder, my head is suddenly a hive of disconnected thoughts, ranging back to the other time I posed for her, in Zabriskie Mansion, just inherited by Bard.

Flashes from the forty years we've had of it together, the tension and the falling-offs, the quiet moments, nights of passion, delusions, illusions, and, with our children, the great hungry city, the endless pressures of money, of a life crying, like the house of D. H. Lawrence's rocking-horse loser, "There must be more money." How well I remember the tug and strain of money. Checks bounced. Borrowing to the last nickel of my credit. Borrowing from Crown, my employer, and Hunter College, shackling myself to them; and I tried to keep writing, to let Mari paint, to keep the children from slipping off the edge of the universe into pool hall or mediocrity.

And then, suddenly, all the decades gone and we are here on the bench and I am still in love and still love to fuss around rivers and have written twenty-odd books, if you include some without my name on them.

I remember taking all the children to school, able to hold the hands of only two, Charles racing across Seventy-ninth, between cars headed in opposite directions, my heart pounding out of my chest. I remember a thousand discrete moments with these children—so various, so challenging, from whom I've learned so much, who have given me so much to love, to admire.

I AM A dowdy fellow, as far from fashion and glamour as one might get, and I think of Marlene Dietrich's pronouncement: "Glamour is assurance." (Just what I'm full of.) "It is a kind of knowing that you are all right in every way, mentally and physically"—how then?—"and in appearance"—me?—"and that whatever the occasion or the situation, you are equal to it." The comment astounds me. Glamour? It is what changes in an hour, like taste, like the aura of the Sphinx, not the Sphinx itself. Glamour? I'm lucky to be here, to finish each day, and though I might admire the lilting elegance of Astaire, that throaty confidence of Dietrich, who mostly thought herself "all right in every way" and in the end wouldn't have others know otherwise, what I know, in my bones, is the stutter of my heart, the grunting struggle to understand what has happened, what is happening to me, the rage to feel, to say, against the tug of a recalcitrant tongue, a perplexed brain. Many years ago, art said to me, like Rilke's archaic torso of Apollo, "You must change your life." I tried. I beat the hesitant words into stories and poems and in despair threw them out. I found little capacity to invent. The world in which I lived was too strange, palpable, evanescent, terrifying to need another. For mortal enemy I always had the IRS; for fear, a child running between two cars or, due home, heading for the Middle East or Morocco instead; and for anxiety, money, always money—enough to pay the rent, cover the check I wrote last week, yesterday, meet tuition. Sometimes I felt like Chardin's visceral, haunting, smiling ray fish, hung on a hook, sliced open, the cat ready to pounce, with varied sea creatures opened too, the knife nearby.

I STILL TAKE my emotional temperature a couple of times each hour. And I must he a hedonist of the first water for loving this pursuit of brown trout on spring creeks so much.

So, sitting near the window, looking at Sphinx Mountain and at my frizzy-haired wife, thinking of days past, landscapes, brush and canvas, East and West, this and that, my unaccountable love of fishing, I suddenly start scribbling away on one of the yellow notepads I always keep handy.

Mari does not look away from the canvas or from me but asks, with some irritation, what I am working on so ferociously.

Must I do everything with such intensity? I tell her it's a chapter in a little book about my odd secret life writing fishing books. The chapter is called "Bergman in Brooklyn."

"Ingmar?" she asks, without looking up.

"Ray!"

"You sure are scribbling hard. Noisy, too."

"I am the Balzac of the bench!" I announce.

"Sure," she says, making certain that she never flatters me neither in word nor in image. "You make Balzac look like Abraham Lincoln."

THIS NEW HOUSE we're in a few years later is a freakish place—a squarish old stone structure, built many years ago to generate power from nearby Blaine Spring Creek, to sell to the few other houses on the bench. Generations of houseflies have nested in the spaces between the rocks that are the walls. The powerhouse is only a short walk from the Downing House and it does not have the same view, though the Sphinx is visible from one of the long thin windows in the living room, and from any of several slight rises in the land in front of the house. A local kitchen-and-bathroom-fixture salesman bought it more than a dozen years ago and appears to have used whatever spare fixtures were available, what he could get at a bargain price—or else he had a weird sense of design. Except for a huge, well-turned, modern kitchen, the fixtures are quirky in the extreme, a garish mixture of kitschy brass, rooms that wouldn't be out of place in the cheapest motels in town, color found chiefly in cathouses.

None of that matters. The main room is thirty or more feet

high, and we like space. Blaine Spring Creek—tumbling too fast to fish—is out back and there are three ponds cantilevered behind the house, the highest taking water from the creek and passing it to the middle pond, and the lowest returning it to Blaine. From the bedroom over the kitchen extension, we can hear the rushing creek all night, and if we lean out those windows we can see the ponds, often with trout rising.

I have my four fly rods, vests, boots, and jackets on nails in the garage, near the woodpile, on which I've placed twenty-odd fly boxes and other paraphernalia; Mari keeps all of her art supplies out there, too, on the large wooden tool table. She paints only outside, except now and then when it's windy and she works in the open garage. We were here last autumn for a few weeks and she painted the umber hayfields on the Varney Road and the autumn colors behind Doc Losee's house—alizarin, crimson, the tawny reds of horse chestnuts, which reminded me of upstate New York and the season I first fell in love with this remarkable woman, my first love. The fishing was poor. I floated the Madison with Vaughan several times and came up nearly empty. I know now that something called whirling disease has killed a large proportion of the rainbow trout, though the browns—always my favorites—are apparently immune.

We've been here a week and I've been working steadily at a table I set up near the front door. With masking tape, Mari has put three watercolors on the stone walls of the main room and has just started her first oil. The work is different, and I am watching it carefully. Now and again a doe and her two spotted fawns slip tentatively across the field in front of me, headed for high green grasses near the pond. Twice I heard a clicking sound, like pebbles thrown hard against tin, and found outside a trembling flicker, its neck broken from having flown full force into a window. I gave one bird to a friend, to make flies from; another I left where it fell and within an hour some creature had recycled the feckless bird.

The deaths of the flickers trouble me not at all. I've seen enough death over the past years and it has rather gotten into my blood that death comes for the archbishop and Ivan Ilyich and every little and large thing in its own time. Like Everyman, I don't care to be forward about it myself, and several years ago almost slipped away. I had been feeling weak for a month and had attributed it merely to a bit too much work, a bit of age, the onset of still more weight after a severe weight loss. Then one day at lunch with a pleasant fellow I'd wanted for a year to meet, I raised a fork and barely had the strength to hold it up. A day later, after my doctor diagnosed the problem as the flu, I passed out and was hauled to the hospital feetfirst with a failing pulse, jaundice, a clogged bile duct—all from a gallbladder that had gone berserk. After eleven days on intravenous antibiotics my various organs calmed down enough so the surgeons could pluck out my gallbladder, which they said had been "fried to my liver."

And then Mari developed alarming symptoms: periodic bouts of severe abdominal pain, total nausea, and radical weight loss. She took batteries of tests, then more batteries of unpleasant tests, then got widely varying diagnoses, and switched doctors a few times; one doctor called me paranoid for wanting to see the CAT scans; another shouted at Mari; all, after a lifetime of good health, seemed like mere money-grubbing technicians to me. Just before we came out she finally had abdominal surgery to remove tumors. But the pains and weight loss continued, the CAT scans found more tumors. We considered canceling our Montana trip that summer, but Mari insisted. Now she lay in bed, with Sphinx Mountain looming out the window. Old Doc Losee from down the road came over. He touched and listened with naked ear; he dropped to the floor beside her bed and listened more, his ear to her spleen. A half hour later he spotted a neck goiter that all the New York specialists had missed. It surely means hyperthyroid disease, which probably accounts for her severe weight loss. That, at least, is treatable, and the tumors have all proved benign. Every surgeon in New York has wanted to operate and we—and Losee—resist such quick-draw artists. Mari says: "They look at my ovaries and see their next trip to Caracas." Losee stayed two hours, the last hour to be sure *I* was all right, and then I walked him outside at one-twenty and he paused to show me the Milky Way and half a dozen constellations. Just like the New York doctors would have done.

So we're feeling a touch of mortality this summer and we're sticking close to this big old house. We still watch the Sphinx and Mari has painted it, but she is becoming more and more interested in the ponds, with their overhanging branches, deadfalls and dying trees, reflections, and patches of light. She had been working steadily behind the powerhouse, facing the creek, and on the rim of the ponds. Here in the West, without boundaries, she was at first attracted to the vastness of the place, buffered by a dozen different skies each hour, the light, the sense that we are both smaller and larger here, that all is in flux—even the mountain, surely the cloud formations and colors in the sixty-mile sky, and the colors the sky imputes to slope and field, water and mountain peak. Now the ponds, which are more intimate, contained, even magical, combine all she has sought here.

As I sit here she walks onto the mound beside the pond, sets up her easel, fixes the canvas, squeezes out her paints upon a long sheet of wax paper, and starts still again from white. Her movements are at first tentative, as if she is still not fully incarnate, as if she's a guest in her body. Her loss of thirty pounds had made her wraithlike. But as she adjusts the easel slightly, then adjusts it again, then fixes a section of this new vista in her eye, she becomes more deliberate, marking the pond and the bent tree in her mind, the innumerable reflections and shadows, then fixing shapes related to those two forms onto the canvas with several bold strokes of her brush, touched with ochre. Warm colors next to cool next to warm. Push and pull. The reflections endemic to water, not to earth. Always she wants the whole. Now she is more fully herself; now she enters that dance, that triangle between her, the world, and the canvas, and becomes fully alive in her intensity, even as she struggles not to *express* something but to make the recalcitrant canvas take wing, breathe, and sing.

THEN, ALL TOO soon, it is time to leave this place where we came to transact some private business. We were not here for very long but we were here together, and we have tried to be good friends to this country that we have come to love, to take it inside us and to leave it alone.

Before I pack for the trip home, I take a hard look at the canvases she has made this summer—eighteen of them, and three portfolios of watercolors—ready to be crated and shipped UPS from the True Value store in Ennis. To my left, below the Gravellies, is the pond that Mari has been painting; it is contained, more intimate than most of Montana, but it has its lien on wildness, too. And the paintings of the pond are full of light and shadow, reflection and evanescence. I have not learned everything but I have learned some things about her paintings.

Across the valley, then the river, then another bench, and on above the foothills, there is Sphinx Mountain. It's still there. It looks solid as rock. But it's having one of its red days.

14

AT THE POND

More and more this past spring and summer I have found myself sitting near the sorry little pond I built on this Catskill hillside. Before its construction, a fisheries expert came and took soil samples, tested the pH, estimated the fecundity of the few springs; he warned me at once that it would draw too little water and that the rocky soil was porous. He said the pond would depend on road runoff, which would be filled with car grime and toxic road salts. What could survive in that?

The technical reports supported his views, bleakly. Only the pH was marginally okay. Several contractors had their doubts and refused the business.

We had bought a summerhouse in Woodstock with some of the cash we got from the sale of the publishing business—a house built by Fletcher Martin, Mari's second art teacher in California, when she was fifteen. We more than doubled the size of the studio and Mari adored the space. I took a large room for an office and filled it with books and paintings. Winters were raw but every spring brought a riot of color when all was in bloom—the lilac, the great magnolia tree, the three weeping cherry trees, all the pinks and purples and the spears of green that became golden jonquils. We loved the place and had never worked better. We celebrated my seventy-fifth birthday and then our fiftieth anniversary here a decade earlier, and all of our grown kids came—Paul, a professor at the University of Hawaii then; Charlie, a filmmaker; Jenny, a literary agent; and Tony, now founder and publisher of a large publishing firm. Those with children brought them and we all spent Thanksgivings and noisy Christmases here. Paul flew in from Hawaii, with Monica, his partner. He had not yet contracted melanoma. There is a photograph of all of us at the anniversary celebration—the motley, maverick, beautiful, smiling tribe of us.

I had been mad for having a pond, some water of my own, to hold a few fish, to float my few acres of hillside. I looked carefully at ponds built by several neighbors: my friend Bill's pond had dozens of springs and held a dozen huge trout; another, with a firm bentonite bottom, was always full. Mari said I had a bad dose of pond envy, and I did. So in the end, smarter than my experts, I deluded myself into believing none of them, just as I had once not believed the teachers who'd said I could not rise from the pit I'd dug for myself or become reasonably literate, and found a genial contractor no more optimistic than the others but willing to take a chance if I was. He promised nothing, and I accepted that. So he set up his retired father on the backhoe for a week and I watched with satisfaction and hope as the old man chugged in and out of the hole, building a swale for the road runoff and a berm to contain the water, carving out of the rocky soil an amoeba-shaped area while in the corner of his mouth chewing and smoking the cigar his wife never let him enjoy at home, a quiet smile on his face, man and machine indefatigable, one.

The local building inspector, though he approved my plan, shook his head and insisted there was no hope for the pond and called it in his report "a seasonal hole." With the unreliable water source on my brain, I offered my neighbor Fisher the chance to sell me a quarter acre of his eighteen, a spot thick with fallen trees and an active swamp; but we could only negotiate for me to sink a pump into his wet hollow and thus gain a few drinks of cold water for the fish now and then.

It was not your dream pond. But it filled with the heavy spring rains—and it was actually ninety feet across at the longest length, longer than I could cast a fly. So I promptly stocked it with bluegills from Bill's pond and Bill was hopeful enough to add three foot-long largemouth bass and a half dozen rainbow trout. When all these survived not only the first late-summer drought but the frozen winter, I became emboldened and added a ten-inch grass carp, three koi, a few of Bill's golden shiners, more bluegills, and a bucket of emerald shiners and sawbellies from a local bait shop. At least the bass and trout would get a decent meal now and then before they froze or boiled.

The bluegills made their pancake beds that second May and soon there were dozens of bluegill fingerlings and several bass fry. A few years later some ten-inch bass appeared, so that family was growing. The trout grew fat, lasted three years, and then vanished en masse after an August heat wave. Friends added six orfes, a red Russian fish, and some turtles, but the turtles didn't like the murky soup, stayed only a year or so and then left for more accommodating homes or died. I got two dozen tadpoles from the bait shop and later heard a few frogs. Then they disappeared, perhaps with help from the local blue heron or the mink I saw one afternoon. When two of the koi vanished, I bought another, which thrived as a sidekick to the one I'd put in earlier, by then a full seven or eight pounds. The carp, with an appetite as great as mine, kept the pond clear of algae and could occasionally be seen nibbling on overhanging bushes.

The pond still doesn't hold its water any better than I can, and after a gully washer it's often the color of coffee flushed with milk. Even low and distressed it is never even faintly clear. But now, in its sixteenth year, it is still alive and hosts a stew of vigorous denizens: one plump bass, far too many hungry, stunted bluegills, the two bright koi, four orange orfes, sawbellies galore, and the gigantic triploid grass carp—black, magisterial, ugly, slow. The miracle is that anything survives in the unpromising waters.

I like to sit on the dock in the heavy dusk and toss food pellets or pieces of bread to who will have them. Sometimes I think of Nat, Rose, Arthur, or Amie, and a fire, and classrooms and offices and books and a tiny, snot-green room in Greenwich Village, and sometimes I think of Ice Pond, which I first fished more than three-quarters of a century ago, a close friend or two, and fish in the murky waters of my past. And always now I think of Mari and Paul.

MARI DIED SEVERAL years ago, a few months after our fifty-eighth anniversary. She had given me life. She had been my life. We had loved with passion, sometimes fought when someone said something in the heat of then. Shared without reserve. I think of dumb arguments, flashes of anger, how I could not sleep except beside her, how we laughed and worked and loved, and did not mind silences and finished each other's sentences or did not need to do so. There was a banter that bound us and now is gone. The night of her last exhibition in Chelsea, she felt excruciating pain in her right femur and could barely walk. The MRI showed that her old breast cancer had wandered to her bone and that led to a painful operation, some wild hopes, six months of radiation and physical therapy, some moments of genuine hope, and then a horrible decline. She died in April and I was devastated. Nearly two years later, I was driving on the River Road after dropping Charlie at the Rhinecliff train station and suddenly could not breathe. I stopped abruptly on the shoulder, put my head in my hands, shouted like a trapped animal, and began to cry bitterly. I had barely cried since my days at the boarding school. I must have stayed that way for half an hour, weeping.

And then, two years almost to the day of Mari's death, Paul died of the melanoma he had fought for a dozen years. Both had died when the forsythia was golden at the transverse I crossed every day to see each in the hospital. Only the French word *arrachement* comes to mind when I think of them—a raw ripping away, like that of a tree torn by a storm, leaving a gaping hole.

I READ AND remember less, perhaps understand a bit more. Mostly these past years I have tried to cobble together bits of my fractured days, looking for hints of the pattern, the arc of it all. I have tried to find a few of its meanings, make some order out of the disparate days. For my memory, which buoyed me for so many years after I found it, has been slipping downstream, vanishing—names, whole passages of favorite prose and poetry, now only vaguely in my head, in pieces: books read, even their titles forgotten, words said in a classroom vaporized. We write, says Sándor Márai, "what we have to lose," and I'm probably trying to hold back whatever I have to lose—the dramatic change when I chose life, the start of a family, the years in classrooms and offices, all the shaggy fish tales I wrote, books I published by others, my wife and children. Memory is fugitive, capricious. I remember what I can, prompted by a sight, a photograph, a word, a smell.

I am flooded with questions I cannot answer. Whether my whole life was set on iron rails that raw March night before I was born, when a young husband developed pneumonia and a few days later died. And, if so, whether his "good heart" killed him, or something my mother said or thought she said, or carelessness, or a belief in the invincibility of youth, or bad chance. And what difference does that make for me now? Surely my mother in all her shock and grief and guilt never imagined traveling her lonely road, surrounded by so many who did not love her, and surely set ripples in motion in my life. Ripple after widening ripple—all many years ago. And when those ripples played out, others began, until those too vanished. Or was the beginning in that little room where I first shook my life by the throat and sought whatever I could find, blindly, only vaguely suspected? Was the life already crouched inside me, like the heart of a bulb, or was it newly built, of air? There were quickenings. But as the world's great events spun past me—war, social and technological change, riot—the worlds I most regarded were my large beloved family, my books, and myself. I have no theory about this. I have fewer and fewer theories and have grown to distrust all ideologies. Too often I see the other side of all equations. I have broken with half a dozen old friends for reasons I don't remember or understand, keep new ones to my heart, reconcile with old ones, have found new loyalties in the kaleidoscope of change. I cherish yearly Seders with great friends; they remind me of my grandfather's, though my Hebrew is no better. I lean away from the piscatorial prose I loved and have been so grateful for, toward prose far from moving water, which is harder. I think of this little whaling voyage by one Nick.

Tonight, in the heavy evening dusk, I take a long look at our huge living and dining room before I head yet again to the pond. Once, many years ago, on the River Road, we faintly imagined such a house as this: paintings leaning against chairs and tables, even covering bookcases, and books everywhere— endless numbers and configurations of books, piled on chairs, benches, tables, cramming every bookcase, on the floor, in the bathrooms, in my large book-lined office, in unopened boxes from used-book dealers, books glanced at, considered, read slowly. And the happy mix of things bought by Mari, who loved "things," at rummage sales or bazaars, a few at a local auction—scores of ceramics, a rampant wooden horse, candelabras, African masks and an African spoon man, a grandfather clock that keeps fair time, Indian statuettes, posters by Klee, Matisse, Picasso, a few original; a little stone "Metzan man" Mari bought in her teens, which we placed on a mantelpiece wherever we moved. Mostly books and paintings—and a slew of children and grandchildren visiting, all always a bit older, and always memories of a woman who stayed the course with this old mumbler for fifty-eight years, through great passion and ice and some shouting and a mountain of love, and who followed her own destiny with intrepid persistence. She was here and she is gone, and Paul is gone, and their absences are raw and pungent and their memories precious. Everything and its placement shouts her presence. And every day still more books arrive, and every day messages from the children, and sometimes from their children, who will soon have their own lives to fashion. Sometimes I look at an old photograph on my desk, of our children when they were perhaps six to ten, and sometimes I see glimmers there of who they became. Sometimes I look closely at a photograph taken at a nearby hotel some years ago, at our fiftieth anniversary; there are thirteen of us, most looking in different directions. Ah, the great mulch of it, the textured stew. How much richer and fuller a life than we conjured in our wildest imaginings. How different from that tiny room.

Tonight I lumber back from the pond—a bear of a man, garrulous, bearded, often impatient with myself, walking with a rolling gait and a cane, with titanium hips and too much belly. A great athlete I once played basketball with remembers me as "a skinny little kid from Brooklyn who could run all day." I barely know that boy anymore and don't much miss him. He was there and I am here.

I pass Mari's studio and again see her starting a new very large canvas, with the image of a carousel horse. I know something about her, about the mystery of us. I pause for a few moments and look in the window at the large studio we built, where I have been sorting, donating, distributing the vast amount of work Mari left—still filled with paintings, easels, taborets, props like the carousel horse or the large carving of an Ibibio woman Mari called Gertrude, ceramic pots, plates, a smorgasbord of still-life objects, and I see her laying in some charcoal lines on the large new canvas, larger than she is, beginning again.

In the darkened glass of the studio, suddenly mirrorlike, I catch a glimpse of an old fellow with a beard and uncombed hair; he looks a little like a badly tied trout fly, but not someone who once thought he had no life. I smile. I cannot find any of that devastating self-knowledge Gabriel finds in the mirror of Joyce's story. I see a runneled face, an aging man still in love with words and a handful of people, still with much work to do, important to him. The old fire I found in me, that sustained me, is banked low, but the orange coals are bright.

Back at the pond, a doe appears; she watches me for a moment, sizing up possible danger that she need not fear, and when I move slightly she bounds with grace across the low stone wall.

There is a noise below me, in the sloping field, a whirring of wings. It is merely a flock of crows rising from the high grasses, making the air tremulous in their departure, like all those years of fear and doubt and striving, of joy and love, rising, fluttering, and then, in a crazy crowd, gone.

Nick Lyons has lived a full, varied, and fascinating life—flush with contrasts. He has a B.S. degree from the prestigious Wharton School of Finance and Commerce and holds a Ph.D in the vastly different field of literature, from the University of Michigan. He has written some twenty-odd books and hundreds of essays on such diverse topics as an obscure New England poet who believed all of his poems were dictated by the Holy Spirit, dieting, the Sony Corporation, and fly fishing. His essays have appeared in *The New York Times, Harper's, National Geographic, Field & Stream, Outdoor Life, Big Sky Journal, The Pennsylvania Gazette,* and widely elsewhere. He was a college basketball player, an English professor at Hunter College for twenty-six years, Executive Editor at Crown Publishers, and founder and publisher of The Lyons Press. A noted fly fisherman, Lyons was awarded the prestigious Arnold Gingrich Award, The Anglers' Club's Medal of Honor, and he was inducted into the Fly Fishing Hall of Fame. Lyons was married for fifty-eight years to the late painter Mari Lyons and their family includes four children and four grandchildren. He lived in Woodstock, New York, for many years and now lives in New York City.